Napoleon in America:
Essays in Biography & Popular Culture

Nov. 16, 2015

*For my dear friend Betty Lee -
I hope you enjoy adding my book
to your library! With best wishes always,*
Tom Vance

Foreword by Sara Heil

Illustration by Rebecca Sinclair

Copyright © 2012 Tom Vance

Revised May 2013

All rights reserved.

ISBN-13: 978-1466489301

DEDICATION

For my wife Kathy

and for those history teachers who most inspired me:

John Fannin,
The Stanley Clark School, South Bend, Indiana

John Schutz,
John Adams High School, South Bend, Indiana

Albert Castel,
Western Michigan University, Kalamazoo, Michigan

CONTENTS

Foreword

1 Napoleon USA 1
2 The Faint Echo 11
3 Crafting the Life 23
4 The Publishers 39
5 American Best-Seller 50
6 Teaching Napoleon 64
7 Chronology 77
8 The Art of Napoleon 92
Notes 101
Acknowledgments 125

Cover Illustration
by Rebecca Sinclair

Charcoal pencil drawing after the 1894 lithograph by New York City artist James Fagan (1864-1940), after the portrait by Jean-Baptiste Greuze (1725-1805). Greuze painted 22-year-old First Lieutenant Bonaparte in 1791 while Napoleon was stationed in Valance with the Fourth Regiment of Artillery. See the Notes section for details.

FOREWORD

It is with great honor that I share a few words about how perfectly suited Tom Vance is to be the author of this book, *Napoleon in America*. Although Napoleon never actually walked on American soil, this book is about the fascinating internationally renowned historical figure, Napoleon Bonaparte, and his incredible influence and presence in America.

For several years, I have invited Tom to speak to my third-year French students about the wide influence that Napoleon has in the world. Each year, without hesitation, he presents with great enthusiasm and shares his passion, knowledge, and unique perspectives on a topic that is virtually impossible to cover within a fifty-minute class period with at least thirty high school sophomores. He accomplishes this seemingly impossible task with success and grace every time for he knows how to make Napoleon's story come to life for my students as well as his many other audiences.

Several of these students then had the opportunity to travel to France with me during the summer to see first-hand the many monuments and references to Napoleon that Tom mentioned during his presentation. They analyzed the two different paintings of Napoleon's coronation in both the Louvre and in the palace of Versailles and they marveled at the marble tomb in which

Napoleon rests at Les Invalides. They were by far the most appreciative group of American teenagers regarding the historical significance of Napoleon Bonaparte.

Throughout the year, most of the conversations between Tom and I end up being about Napoleon in some way, shape, or form. For this connection, I am forever grateful as I, too, love and appreciate history and all things French. I am proud to be able to have met inspiring folks like Tom Vance whether it be traveling around the world or working in Portage or Bridgman, Michigan.

As for everyday life in Michigan, Tom's wife Kathy has no choice but to follow along this 'Napoleonic journey' that has clearly chosen Tom as much as he has been drawn to it. The library of Napoleon-related articles and books in Vance's possession is frankly impressive, and he frequently acquires new Napoleonic objects, documents, and photos to add to this extensive collection and enhance his studies.

Bravo, Tom, for your passion and dedication to history via biography. You make Napoleon's life accessible and intriguing to many people in your path. We will always remember Napoleon's powerful influence on both a world and local scale. We owe our knowledge and appreciation of historical awareness to you.

~Sara Heil

1
NAPOLEON USA

Adapted from the presentation "Napoleon in Kalamazoo: A Search for his Presence in American Popular Culture" presented at the Michigan Academy of Science, Arts & Letters on March 7, 2008, at Western Michigan University, Kalamazoo.

"The astounding magic of his name in the United States is partly due to a quality of the American mind which makes its possessor the passionate and indiscriminating adorer of greatness in every form." – William Milligan Sloane [1]

"What America admires in Napoleon is the typical American…In all these respects – militarism, autocratic efficiency, parvenu display, self-advertisement, insatiable ambition, gambling-mania – America admires Napoleon as a hero of legend, but follows the precepts and example of Washington." – Albert Leon Guerard [2]

While these comments by Professors Sloane and Guerard are now dated (1910 and 1924 respectively), Napoleon is everywhere in America and this essay seemed to be an appropriate introduction for this collection about his presence in America. Like anyone writing or teaching about Napoleon, the amount of available sources is overwhelming.

Therefore, the goal of this little book is not to follow the many trails of Napoleon across America, but to focus on these few topics which stirred my interest over the last several years. Having said that, here are some examples to help illustrate the connection he continues to have on our country, from mainstream and social media to towns in the Midwest.

The online feature, "Huff Post Live" from Los Angeles on December 4, 2012, featured a panel on how to solve Europe's financial crisis, and one of the teasers promoting the segment was the question: Does Europe need another Napoleon? The discussion pondered what it would take to unify Europe politically – something about which Napoleon spent a great deal of his energy. Meanwhile, news anchors often use the name 'Waterloo' when describing someone's personal defeat, without any need to provide historical context. Political commentators discuss the first 100 days of presidential administrations, a measure originating with Napoleon's 100-day reign following his return from exile on Elba to his downfall after Waterloo. We talk about the people with longtime experience in a community, business, or organization as the Old Guard, a reference to the most elite segment of Napoleon's Imperial Guard.

Vanity Fair's March 2012 issue featured a piece, "The Quest for Napoleon," by Martin Scorsese on film historian Kevin Brownlow's restoration of the famed 1927 cinematic masterpiece by Abel Gance about Napoleon's life. The five and a half-hour film was playing that month at the San Francisco Silent Film Festival with a score by Carl Davis performed by the Oakland East Bay Symphony – "a major event," says Scorsese. Meanwhile, *The New York Times* "Arts & Leisure" section featured a page one review of the restoration, which continued with a full-page on the inside titled "Napoleon is Lost, Long Live Napoleon." According to Manohla Dargis, the festival "is hoping movie lovers will be so tempted by "Napoleon" that they'll pay $40 to $120 a ticket for an event that begins in the afternoon and incorporates three intermissions, including a dinner break." And finally, on the heels of the success of the film "Lincoln," *The Hollywood Reporter* reported in March 2013 that Steven Spielberg was planning a television mini-series on the never-produced movie screenplay about Napoleon by Stanley Kubrick. [3]

And Napoleon is in Las Vegas, of all places. You can find him at the Gold and Silver Pawn Shop, better known as the location of "Pawn Stars," the popular History Channel program. Assistant General Manager Travis Benton reports having had "a few different pieces over the years" and currently had a Steve Kaufman serigraph of Napoleon. During the 2010 season, a customer brought in miniature hand-painted ivory portraits of Napoleon and Josephine, valued at about $800 and receiving $425 for them. And while you're there, you can stop for a visit at the Napoleon restaurant at the Paris casino property and toast to Napoleon's enduring legacy in the shadow of huge portraits of Napoleon and Josephine. You might also stop at Bauman's Rare Books at The Shoppes at the Palazzo to spend any winnings you win on an autograph or leather-bound volume (their flagship store is in New York City, and their other shop is in Philadelphia). [4]

Television viewers also find occasional items linked to Napoleon on Antiques Road Show. In 2005, during the broadcast from Portland, Oregon, Andrew Brunk (senior specialist of decorative arts, folk art, and furniture for Brunk Auctions) appraised a tiger maple desk from 1825 for between $5,000 to $7,000. The guest's family had always called it "The Bonaparte," believing it had belonged to Napoleon's brother Joseph while he was living in Bordentown, New Jersey, at his Point Breeze estate. "I think it's wonderful the way we see pieces of furniture as they move through history; they accumulate this sort of mythology that's attached to them," Brunk told the guest. "And the trick is proving that sort of association." In the end, his assessment was that the desk was probably not at Point Breeze, but the segment provided the chance to tell the story of how Joseph came to America following his brother's defeat at Waterloo. The show from El Paso, Texas, in 2011 featured a sculpture of Napoleon by Jean-Leon Gerome appraised between $8,000-$10,000. [5]

The decorative arts field is filled with Napoleons. The television show, Spin City – running from 1996-2000 and starring Michael J. Fox working in the mayor's office as Mike Flaherty – featured a framed print of Jacques-Louis David's iconic "Napoleon Crossing the Alps" on his office wall intended as a positive image for his character. Years before, in the 1946 film by Frank Capra, "It's A Wonderful Life" starring James Stewart as the good George Bailey, the evil Mr. Potter's office is adorned with a huge dark Napoleon bust while Bailey Savings & Loan is decorated with a portrait of Abraham Lincoln. Hollywood, at least in films we now watch on TCM, often uses Napoleon in set designs, like the statue of Napoleon on horseback on a fireplace mantel in "The Maltese Falcon" (1941, starring Humphrey Bogart) and another Napoleon on horseback on an editor's desk in "Meet John Doe," starring Gary Cooper and Barbara Stanwyck (1941). "Here Comes Mr. Jordan" with Robert Montgomery (1941) features a black bust of Napoleon on a desk in a mansion. "The Rich Are Always With Us" (1932, starring Ruth Chatterton) features a large framed portrait of Napoleon II, from the wonderful painting by British artist Sir Thomas Lawrence.

Readers of the new best-selling biography *Thomas Jefferson: The Art of Power* by Jon Meacham are reading how Jefferson's cherished Monticello's parlor featured (and continues to feature) Napoleon among the many paintings and sculptures decorating the home. [6]

And the virtual market place of eBay has a wide variety of items from busts, statues, old advertisements, posters, prints, and games. One search found the game Waterloo by Parker Games from 1895 with the original price of $1.25 – "the popular new board game" for 2, 3, or 4 young and old players. On YouTube you can find clips of various videos and films about him and he's even on Facebook, with the site "Napoleon in Modern Art," declaring that all contents on the slide show are public with paintings, drawings, prints, and sculptures by contemporary artists. The Early October 2012 catalog from Orvis (Gifts for Men) advertised a battle of Waterloo chess set, hand-decorated polystone resin players and board for $198.

The iconic image also sells. Google "Napoleon Bonaparte," "U.S." and "advertising" and you'll get 6.4 million hits. Garmin ran a fun Super Bowl spot in 2008 showing Napoleon finding the field of battle thanks to this device. Coke ran a television spot in 2010 showing Napoleon and other historic figures (as miniatures) waking up a student in time to take a history exam (which reminds one of the 1989 film "Bill and Ted's Excellent Adventure," where they go back into time to research an assignment and bring Napoleon and other historic characters to their high school – which, in turn, brings to mind the 2004 "Napoleon Dynamite," whose character was not Napoleonic nor explosive).

Courvoisier, "the cognac of Napoleon," has long used his image in their ads. Breguet watches uses his image in its full-page *New Yorker* magazine ads, using the famous painting of the young general by Antoine-Jean Gros (1771-1835), "Bonaparte at the Bridge of Arcola," a romantic or heroic depiction of his first campaign in Italy in 1796. Seattle, Washington, is home to The Napoleon Co., winner of the 2010 Seattle Business magazine's first annual Washington Family Business Award for a small company. Not all companies with Napoleon's name are actually linked to our Napoleon, but this one is and they use his image on their packaging. [7]

You will also find cartoons, especially in the *New Yorker* from time to time. A recent one, appearing in 2010 by Paul Noth, showed Disney characters in a retreat (like Moscow 1812) with Mickey on a horse (as Napoleon) with the caption saying "I was against Russo-Disneyland from the start." If you Google our topic – Napoleon in America – most of the hits refer to Napoleon "and" America, but you will find discussions on the "AlternateHistory.com" forum with some interesting "what ifs" – especially speculation on the interesting course Napoleon's life would have taken had he succeeded in escaping to America. [8]

In Washington, D.C., Bill Truettner, senior curator of paintings and sculpture at the Smithsonian American Art Museum, can speak to the 18 different Napoleon pieces under his charge – gifts made over the years reflecting interest both in French culture but also testimony to Napoleon's image in America. "Napoleon wasn't always considered a bad guy," he says on reflection. He says one of the most interesting pieces in the collection is a collage by Joseph Cornell which includes a painting of Napoleon with two other images. One of the most famous paintings housed in our country is David's "The Emperor Napoleon in his Study" at the National Gallery in Washington, D.C. See Chapter 8 for a sampling of other Napoleonic holdings at selected museums. [9]

And Napoleon is the subject of intrigue, such as whether or not he was murdered by one of his own staff while in exile on St. Helena in the South Atlantic or if an imposter actually died on St. Helena in his place. The 2009 Clive Cussler novel *Spartan Gold* (A Fargo Adventure) begins with Napoleon's crossing of the Alps when his army makes a discovery they are unable to transport so they bury it, identifying the location on wine bottle labels – which leads a present day treasure hunt.

According to historian R. S. Alexander, before the start of the Civil War there were 15 towns or hamlets across the nation named either Napoleon or Bonaparte. This was during a time when students at Harvard annually selected Napoleon as the greatest man in history. Meanwhile, there were people named after Napoleon also, such as Civil War General Napoleon Bonaparte Buford (1807-1883) and Napoleon Bonaparte Broward (1857-1910) who served as governor of Florida. Others had nicknames like P.G.T. Beaurgard, a Confederate general known as "Little Napoleon" and the Union general George McClellan known as "Young Napoleon." [10]

If you're in southern Michigan, driving along Interstate 94, head south between Jackson and Ann Arbor and you'll run into the town and township of Napoleon, in Jackson County, founded in 1830 (head north and you'll run into Waterloo). Abram Bolton, a military man and admirer of Napoleon Bonaparte, suggested the name for the town. Today, the town has a population of 1,200, and the public school system also bears the Napoleon name.

There are other towns, present and past named in his honor: Napoleon, Ohio, is southwest of Toledo, established in 1834, and is the largest U.S. city to bear this name with more than 9,000 residents; Napoleon, Indiana, is southeast of Indianapolis (and on U.S. Highway 421 you'll find Bonaparte's Retreat, a restaurant and lounge that sports a sign outside with an image of Napoleon); and Napoleon, Kentucky, is south of Cincinnati, Ohio. And then there is Napoleonville, Louisiana, south of Baton Rouge, and Bonaparte, Iowa, west of Burlington (there were plans for a village named Napoleon across the river from Bonaparte, but it never took off).

There are Napoleons that have disappeared. Napoleon, Arkansas – at the mouth of the Arkansas River – was founded by Frederick Notrebe, who had served in the French Army before immigrating to America around 1810. The town was damaged during the Civil War, then hit by a flood in 1874, and is no more. Napoleon, Missouri, in the greater Kansas City metro area, is no longer on the map, but that site is a few miles from Wellington and between the two lies a small unincorporated crossroads named Waterloo. Napoleon, North Dakota, southeast of Bismarck, is named after its founder, a Napoleon Goodsill, whom I assume (but could not verify) was named after "our" Napoleon. [11]

There are rooms named after him – back to Michigan now – such as one at The Grand Hotel on Mackinac Island, at the intersection of the Upper and Lower Peninsula's where Lake Michigan and Lake Huron meet. According to its website, the hotel's "most exceptional accommodations" are its named rooms and two-bedroom suites, "all feature their own thematic design, furnishing and ambiance that accurately capture the place, time and lifestyle each of the names suggest." Joining Abraham Lincoln and Theodore Roosevelt among rooms named for national and state celebrities are the Napoleon Suite and Josephine Suite (see photo gallery link at their website). [12] The local history of Three Rivers, Michigan, includes the story of Chas F. Thoms, a Swiss soldier who served in the French Army under Napoleon, moving to the area with his two sons around 1831. Meanwhile, the West Cooper Cemetery in Cooper Township, Michigan, includes the grave site of a resident named Napoleon Bonaparte Reed.

Napoleon is alive and well in Kalamazoo, in southwest Michigan (an hour west of Napoleon, Michigan). Kalamazoo City Hall, constructed in 1931 in art deco style, features a unique mural fresco behind the City Commission dais that lists the Ten Commandments in Hebrew along with a list of great law makers in world history. Designed and painted by local artist Otto Stauffenberg, the mural, named 'Justice,' includes Napoleon among 18 lawmakers beginning with Hammurabi and ending with Michigan's Thomas Cooley, a chief justice of the Michigan Supreme Court. [13]

A few blocks away, crossing through Bronson Park (where Abraham Lincoln once spoke), is the Kalamazoo Valley Museum, operated by Kalamazoo Valley Community College adjacent to the College's downtown campus. Curator of Research Tom Dietz has some interesting items, although not on display when I visited: A glass bottle in Napoleon's image and a pewter plate showing a side view of his head and shoulders were from a 1938 donation by Susan Steben Stark (the decorative plate is by Cde Franz). A bronze bust was donated in 1973 from Ethel Todd Woodams, daughter of Kalamazoo's well-known A. M. Todd family. A two-page handwritten speech about Napoleon is dated February 16, 1850, referring to the audience as "gentlemen" but the venue is not identified, although there is a notation of Little Prairie Ronde, Michigan and the unidentified author is very critical of Napoleon. A business trading card with the image of a boy dressed as Napoleon with a pipe, is most likely an artifact from the tobacco industry, donated to the museum in 1962.

Over at Kalamazoo College's library is the Rare Book collection that began in the 1920s with gifts from the library of Albert May Todd, a prominent Kalamazoo citizen and an internationally known book and art collector (his library contained about 10,000 volumes). Major bequests from A.M. Todd's daughter, Ethel Todd Woodhams, and Elizabeth Dewing Todd, the widow of Todd's son Paul, brought together a major portion of the library originally collected by Todd. The jewel of the collection – relevant to our topic – is the 20-volume set *Description de l'Egypte* (Paris, 1809-1822), resulting from the scientific aspect of Napoleon's campaign in Egypt. The set features 894 large engraved plates, many double-page and folding (72 in color). In 2009, the Rare Book Room held an exhibit titled Napoleon's Egypt: Scenes from the Monumental 'Description de l'Egypte.' [14]

Next door at Western Michigan University's Waldo Library (named after the University's first president), is a Serves vase on loan from the University's permanent art collection with Napoleon scenes. The 35-inch high porcelain vase (untitled, but depicting the battle of Wagram) was a gift in 1932 from the Todd Collection. According to Mindi K. Bagnall, curator of the permanent art collection, "This vase is done in hard-paste porcelain which supplanted soft-paste porcelain after the French Revolution at Sevres. Sevres had been the seat of the royal company of porcelain makers since the 1740s and its wares were known as the finest in France. After the Revolution, the company was reorganized and by Napoleon's time was putting out many large vases like ours, usually in sets which commemorated campaigns and conquests. These large vessels were purely decorative, and many of the larger pieces, like ours, could be revolved in order to see all sides." [15]

Crossing the state line into Indiana reveals an exciting project that illustrates Napoleon's impact on the reading public in a small American town. A collaborative effort among the Muncie Public Library, the Center for Middletown Studies at Ball State University, and the Ball State University Libraries, has resulted in a database and search engine named What Middletown Read. The circulation records of the public library from November 5, 1891 through December 3, 1902 include 25 volumes corresponding to Napoleon, tracking the number of patrons (267) checking out those titles. During this period, G. A. Henty was the most popular author, with his *Through Russian Snows: A Story of Napoleon's Retreat from Moscow* checked out 118 times (another Henty book, *At Aboukir* and *Acre: A Story of Napoleon's Invasion of Egypt* was checked out 30 times). Coming in at second place was *A Boy of the First Empire* by Elbridge Streeter with 67 transactions. The library had four copies of William Sloane's *Life of Napoleon Bonaparte* and five Napoleonic titles by Imbert Saint-Amand. Other titles being read by Muncie library patrons during this time are in the notes. [16]

Napoleon's hold on the American imagination remains strong, topped only by the French themselves. Yes, things have changed since Americans went through 50 editions of T.J. Headley's *Napoleon and His Marshals* in the mid-1800s. American visitors to Paris no longer flock to Napoleon's Tomb as American soldiers and sailors did during WWI, in what one American historian called the "manifestation of Napoleon's popularity throughout America." [17]

Professor David A. Bell, who teaches history at Princeton, has observed that modern historians have typically ignored Napoleon. "To be sure, popular interest in the man remains great – in the past decade, biographies have appeared from major publishers at the rate of more than one per year…Yet *The American Historical Review*, the flagship journal of the profession, has not devoted a single article to Napoleon in thirty years." *The New Republic* book review by Bell of the Napoleon biography by Steven Englund was titled "Just Like

Us." According to Bell, "The ability of ordinary people to identify with Napoleon was also the key to his success." He wrote, "It is somewhat surprising that Napoleon's modern sensibility has attracted so little attention from the recent crop of biographers. But then, while modern, it is not quite our own sensibility." [18]

His name and image, however, remain alive in American life. The following essays examine how Americans have written, read, and thought about Napoleon Bonaparte – and continue to be influenced by this captivating, complicated, and controversial figure.

2
THE FAINT ECHO

Originally published as "The Faint Echo of 19th Century American Napoleonic Biography" on the website "Napoleonic Literature," October 2006.

> "Among the eminent persons of the nineteenth century, Bonaparte is far the best known, and the most powerful; and owes his predominance to the fidelity with which he expresses the tone of thought and belief, the aims of the masses of active and cultivated men...Every one of the million readers of anecdotes, or memoirs, or lives of Napoleon, delights in the page, because he studies it in his own history...He is no saint...and he is no hero, in the high sense. The man in the street finds in him the qualities and powers of other men in the street. He finds him, like himself, by birth a citizen, who, by very intelligible merits, arrived at such a commanding position..." – Ralph Waldo Emerson [1]

Americans shared a number of key historic events with Napoleon Bonaparte during the 19th century: the largest peaceful land transfer in world history with the Louisiana purchase (doubling the size of our nation); the War of 1812, considered by some historians to be a part of the Napoleonic Wars; and the impact of the battle of Waterloo, with Napoleon's plan of fleeing to America and the actual immigration of Bonaparte family members to America, including Napoleon's brother Joseph who lived in New Jersey for 19 years. [2]

While Americans did not admire Napoleon the way they did George Washington, they were captivated by Napoleon's achievements through talent as opposed to birthright like many other European heads of state. Napoleon was celebrated as a self-made man. According to one recent analysis, the fascination with Napoleon (or "the cult of Napoleon") in the U.S. was second only to that in

France. There were plays produced in America about Napoleon as early as 1820 and by 1859 there were 15 towns named Napoleon or Bonaparte. [3]

The American publishing business was aware of this fascination for the former Emperor. In addition to publishing American writings on Napoleon, numerous editions of translated foreign memoirs appeared in American editions primarily from Philadelphia and New York publishing houses. [4] While there were a number of American writers and historians publishing articles and books about Napoleon during the 19th century, this essay focuses on five American writers whose works of Napoleonic biography stood out during this period. Categorized by their professional training, they consisted of two ministers, a lawyer, a professional historian, and a teacher. [5] In addition to describing these authors and their contributions to Napoleonic literature and publishing, this article attempts to show the relevance of these works to Napoleonic historians during the 20th and 21st centuries (see the list at the end of this chapter citing these early American Napoleonic authors).

J. T. Headley

Joel T. Headley (1813-1897), who wrote more than 30 books of biography, history and travel, was the author of three volumes on Napoleon: the two-volume *Napoleon and His Marshals* (1846), *The Distinguished Marshals of Napoleon* (1850), and *The Imperial Guard of Napoleon: from Marengo to Waterloo* (1851). Of these works, his two-volume work on the marshals was his most popular and the one most likely to be referenced in 20th century works. The set was still in print in 1923, issued in cloth at a cost of $1.12 by Haldeman-Julius Company, Girard, Kansas. [6]

Napoleon and His Marshals, published when Headley was 33, was his fourth book, but his first biographical work. The title became a best-seller and continued to be popular for decades. With portions of the book originally published in the *American Review*, the 647-page work contains a 66-page chapter on Napoleon and separate chapters on each of the 23 marshals. His eight-page preface identifies the objective of this volume -- "to clear his character from the aspersions of English historians, and the slanders of his enemies" -- and makes it clear that the book contains no originality "except in the way I have arranged and grouped facts already given to the world." Regarding his methods, he explains that his research included visits to many of the Napoleonic battlefields and he mentions 20 key sources he drew from (none of whom are American historians). [7] A review in *The New Englander & Yale Review* declared that, "This work is the work of the season," calling Headley "a man of undoubted genius," although the reviewer objects to the book's bias for its subject and suggests he turn his "strong and lively" talents to American biography. [8]

Headley, a native of New York State, graduated from Union College, New York, and then attended Auburn Theological Seminary, entering the ministry upon graduation. He soon gave up the ministry, and after taking time off to travel and briefly try newspaper work, he turned to what would be a prolific career as an author. *Napoleon and His Marshals* became the first American authored book published by Baker and Scribner.

"The critics scoffed at Headley's verbosity and questioned his facts and opinions," according to one modern day observer. "But Americans, enamoured of Napoleon the man-of-action and ready to forget the rest, bought the book in unprecedented numbers." Within 15 years of its publication date, *Napoleon and His Marshals* was in its 50th edition. While Headley's books would not qualify today as professional history, for his day "they influenced the public and gave him fame and fortune" and was considered "a historian for his time." [9] According to *American Authors: 1600-1900*, however, while Headley's books were popular and "reached an enormous sale," they were "more on the order of compilations than works of scholarship." [10] Thanks to the web site "Napoleonic Literature," *Napoleon and His Marshals* remains 'in print' with the entirety of the two-volume work available at no cost online. The editor of the site, John Schneider, refers to Headley as belonging to the "apologists" camp of Napoleonic historians [11]

Of Headley's three Napoleonic volumes, only the two-volume set on the marshals is evident in a survey of citations: Alexander, Chandler (*Marshals*) and Macartney.

John S. C. Abbott

John S. C. Abbott (1805-1877) wrote *The History of Napoleon Bonaparte* in 1855 when he was 50. Historian and clergyman, the Maine native graduated from Bowdoin College class of 1825, which included Nathaniel Hawthorne and Henry Wadsworth Longfellow. His only other book directly on Napoleon was *Napoleon at St. Helena*, also published in 1855, but some of his other works included volumes on the French Revolution, Josephine, Joseph Bonaparte, and Napoleon III. [12] Abbott trained for the ministry after Bowdoin and was ordained as a Congregational minister. At the age of 38, however, he joined his three brothers as an instructor in a family enterprise, Abbott's Institute, in New York City. Meanwhile, his wife Jane Williams Bourne assisted him in his research. He returned to Maine in 1853 and began work on his biography of Napoleon, which was first serialized in 37 instalments in *Harper's Review* from 1851 to 1854. [13]

The History of Napoleon Bonaparte began its many faceted run as a book form in 1855. The 1883 edition in two volumes (totalling 1,277 pages) features numerous illustrations by C. E. Doepler sprinkled throughout the work, maps by Jacob Wells, and footnotes -- with further details and sources -- at the bottom of some pages. "The history of Napoleon has often been written by his enemies," declares Abbott in the opening of his preface. "This narrative is from the pen of one who reveres and loves the Emperor." He describes the plan for the work as a "plain narrative of what Napoleon did, with the explanations which he gave of his conduct, and with the record of such well-authenticated anecdotes and remarkable sayings as illustrate his character." Regarding this sources, he states that "every incident here recorded, and every remark attributed to Napoleon, are well authenticated." [14]

A 20th century biographical sketch says that Abbott "praised Bonaparte so lavishly that the book, though successful, greatly antagonized the critics." [15] Meanwhile, the historian George Gordon Andrews comments on Abbott's lack of objectivity by saying that Abbott "revealed something of the lengths to which the Napoleonic legend might go," referring to a passage in Abbott's preface saying that he admired Napoleon because he "abhorred war." [16] Four years after the publication of his Napoleon biography, Abbott travelled to France and became friends with Emperor Louis Napoleon. He returned to the ministry and continued writing his books -- a total of 54 by the end of his 72 years. He has been described as "indefatigable, systematic, a man of high standards and purpose." *American Authors* comments that, "Although his work was widely read in its time, it had no lasting literary influence." [17]

Abbott's biography on Napoleon is cited in: Alexander, Chandler (*Campaigns* and *Dictionary*), P. C. Headley, and Korngold. Technically, his book is now again "in print," re-issued in 2002 as an abridged 112-page book available by an on-demand publisher. Also, excerpts are available online through the Gutenberg Literary Archive. [18]

John C. Ropes

John Codman Ropes (1836-1899), an attorney and military historian, is primarily recognized for his Civil War writings, but his works include two books on Napoleon: *Napoleon the First: A Sketch, Political and Military* in 1885 (a 347-page volume based on lectures he delivered at the Lowell Institute in Boston) and *Campaign of Waterloo* in 1892. Ropes was born in Russia to American parents living in St. Petersburg. After his family returned to Salem, Mass., he graduated from Harvard College, followed by Harvard Law. In addition to the practice of law and his writing, he also served as editor of the *American Law Review* (1866-1869) and founded the Military Historical Society of Massachusetts (1876). He was also a member of the Massachusetts Historical Society, the Harvard Historical Society, and a fellow of the American Academy of Arts and Sciences. [19]

"I have not undertaken to write a new history," Ropes explains in the introduction, "but simply to indicate the lines upon which a new history might be written. The task of rectifying the fundamental notions with which nearly all historians have approached the study of the epoch of Napoleon is the task which I proposed to myself." The book contains nine appendixes (examining a variety of historical questions), maps, and an index (and four pages of advertisements, including Dorsey Gardner's *Quatre Bras, Ligny & Waterloo*). Writing from his Boston home, Ropes says, "It ought to be possible for Americans to arrive at an impartial estimate of the credit and blame which should attach to the chief actors in that famous drama." [20]

Both of Ropes' Napoleonic works are mentioned in Dodge, Gottschalk, and Greer; Fisher cites only his *Campaign of Waterloo*.

William Milligan Sloane

William Milligan Sloane (1850-1928) is the author of the most complete and most authoritative biography of Napoleon written in America during the nineteenth century: *Life of Napoleon Bonaparte*. Written while serving as professor of History at Princeton, the book was first published when he was 45 years old as a series in *The Century Magazine* during 1895 and 1896, followed by publication in four oversized volumes in 1896 (totalling 1,149 pages). The work was revised and expanded for the 1912 library edition (totalling 1,876 pages), by which time he was serving on the faculty at Columbia University.

Sloane graduated from Columbia College in 1868 and served for four years on the faculty of the Newell Institute in Pittsburgh, Penn. He studied philosophy, the classics, and the Semitic languages at University of Berlin and then at University of Leipsic. While living in Berlin he worked as a research assistant for American historian and U. S. envoy to the German Court, George Bancroft. With the title of personal secretary, Sloane assisted with the tenth volume of Bancroft's *History of the United States*. Sloane completed his doctorate at the University of Leipsic in 1876. He was a member of several professional societies while studying in Germany and in 1877 he wrote *The Poet Labid: His Life, Times, and Fragmentary Writings*.

Sloane taught history at Columbia where he earned his L.H.D. in 1887 and earned his LL.D. at Rutgers in 1898. He served as editor of both the *Political Science Quarterly* and of the *American Historical Review* and was president of the National (later American) Historical Association and also head of the National Institute of Arts and Letters. While the *Life of Napoleon Bonaparte* is considered his greatest achievement of authorship, he wrote nine other books of biography, history and government, including a volume on the French Revolution. [21]

Writing in the preface to the library edition of *Life of Napoleon Bonaparte* (1910) from New York, Sloane writes, "Judging from the sales, it has been read by many tens if not hundreds of thousands of readers; and it has been extensively noticed in the critical journals of both worlds." While the collection features a complete bibliography, it does not include footnotes, but he explains that he does list references at the beginning each chapter "for those who desire to extend their reading; experts know their own way." Regarding footnotes, he writes that while he has had "extensive correspondence with my fellow workers, there has come to me in all these years but a single request for the source of two statements, and one demand for the evidence upon which certain opinions were based." [22]

This edition, also four volumes, but of traditional size, featured a three-page section on historical sources, a 46-page bibliography and a cumulative index totalling 172 pages. Sloane notes in his historical sources section -- consisting of unpublished documents, published official papers, and contemporary memoirs -- that since he originally wrote this biography that "great numbers of what were then manuscript journals, memoirs, or letters have been printed and published. He notes that proper use has been made of these new sources, and adds, "The author may be pardoned for remarking that few details of importance have been found incorrect, wherever experts agree, and that his many critics have made no demand for the reconstruction of his characterization in its broad outlines, however opposed they may be to his portrayals or discussions." [23]

Sloane's work is complimented in several key references. David G. Chandler refers to Sloane as "the great historian." Yale University Professor of History Edward Gaylord Bourne, wrote in his 1903 edition of August Fournier's 1885 *Napoleon the First: A Biography* that, "The most important general biographies of Napoleon that have appeared in English since Fournier" are Sloane and J. H. Rose, a British author writing in 1902. Albert Guerard wrote in 1924 that the modern reader would be apt to be familiar with Sloane's work, and in 1956 he wrote that Sloane is "among the best-known" authors. [24]

Other references citing Sloane are Chandler (*Dictionary*), Delderfield, Dodge, Greer (noted as a "most valuable" source), Gottschalk, Haythornthwaite, Rose, and Young. The editor of Napoleonic Literature website, John Schneider (Master Sergeant, U.S. Army, retired), has made a CD of the original 1896 volumes available and calls this collection "an epic achievement in the realm of Napoleonic literature." Schneider writes that, "Sloane knew his subject well and, in this work, you will discover a wealth of information that is difficult or impossible to find elsewhere." [25]

Ida Tarbell

Ida M. Tarbell (1857-1944), author of 25 books, wrote one book on Napoleon: *A Short Life of Napoleon Bonaparte* (1895) -- a book that saw several editions -- and edited one volume on Napoleon: *Napoleon's Addresses: Selections from the Proclamations, Speeches and Correspondence of Napoleon Bonaparte* (1897), and wrote the foreword for Mabell S. C. Smith's *The Story of Napoleon* (1928). Tarbell's biography of Napoleon began as a serial in *McClure's Magazine* in 1894. The cover of the first instalment boasts at the top of the page, "A Great Pictorial Life of Napoleon," along with the teaser in the middle of the cover accompanying an illustration of Napoleon, "A New Life with an almost exhaustive series of Napoleon Portraits and over 100 other pictures begins in this number." [26]

The work is introduced by Napoleonic art collector Gardiner G. Hubbard who supplied the majority of art. The work was significant primarily because of the collection of illustrations, many of which were published for the first time. The series, appearing in the three-year old magazine, was credited with significantly increasing circulation. The following year her work appeared as a collection titled *McClure's Complete Life of Napoleon*, a 248-page magazine supplement with all 250 illustrations and issued again in 1896 as *A Short Life of Napoleon Bonaparte* (complete with a Bonaparte family tree and a useful chronology). Although not an authority on the subject of Napoleon, Tarbell conducted her research in Washington, D.C., at the Library of Congress. While she considered her scholarship sketchy, "the public loved the series," according to a recent literary critique. Tarbell's writing is described as "fast-paced, accurate, and informative." [27]

Tarbell graduated from Allegheny College, Pennsylvania, a small liberal arts school in 1880 with a biology degree, and was the only woman in her freshman class. She began her career as a teacher at Poland Union Seminary in Ohio. After three years she decided to leave teaching for journalism and took a position working for the magazine *Chautauguan*. Then, at the age of 33, she went to Paris to study historiography at the Sorbonne and used the Bibliotheque Nationale for her research on French Revolutionary activist Madame Marie Jeanne Roland. She supported herself as a freelance writer for American newspapers, which brought her to the attention of *McClure's Magazine*. She accepted a job offer from that publication in 1893 and returned to the United States. [28]

Following her first book, the Napoleon biography, she quickly became a prolific writer, publishing *Madame Roland: A Biographical Study* and *The Early Life of Abraham Lincoln* in 1896, the two-volume *Life of Abraham Lincoln* in 1900 and by 1905, the work she is often most remembered for, the two-volume exposé, *History of the Standard Oil Company*. Her 1900 study of Lincoln remained a standard work on the former president until 1947, in spite of the refusal by Lincoln's son, Robert Todd Lincoln, to provide access to the family papers. [29] Identified as an historian, journalist and biographer, Tarbell "developed her skills as a biographer, utilizing historical documents to create psychological portraits of her subjects. Her biographies of Napoleon and Lincoln were considered among the most accessible, well-crafted, and thoroughly documented of their time." [30]

According to Tarbell biographer Mary E. Tomkins, Tarbell's central purpose in the Napoleon biography was more historical than biographical, "exploiting the public's curiosity about Napoleon to teach history…" Tomkin writes that Tarbell's "skill in simplifying masses of data and her swift narrative style assured the popularity of the biography." Tomkins writes that in contrast to Sloane's "leisurely biography that was running concurrently in the Century, hers moved swiftly, often changing focus to feature historical highlights rather than meticulously developing the background of their emergence." [31]

In her memoirs, Tarbell – who refers to her life of Napoleon as "a sketch" – concludes that Napoleon's life was "an amazing record of achievement." While she admits that when initially asked to write this life she thought the idea was "laughable," but decided "how could I refuse?" McClure's started her at $40 a week and she was still receiving royalty checks at the writing of her memoirs in 1939. [32]

It is interesting to note that Tarbell recorded the favourable responses she received from John Ropes and William Sloane on her Napoleon. According to Tarbell, Ropes "liked the treatment" and invited her to Boston for lunch, at which time she also had the opportunity to view his Napoleon collection. Regarding Sloane, she wrote that, "A bit of consolation for my hasty work came from the last source I would have expected." When she once complimented Sloane on his Napoleonic scholarship, he replied, "I have often wished that I had had, as you did, the prod of necessity behind me, the obligation to get it out at a fixed time, to put it through, no time to idle, to weigh, only to set down. You got something that way – a living sketch." [33]

Of all the 19th century works included in this survey, only Gottschalk cited Tarbell's Napoleonic biography as a reference.

Conclusion

The advances made in the historical method from the 1840s with Headley and the 1890s with Sloane is evident in Sloane's work and its reception by 19th century historians. The majority of 20th century works citing these five early authors appear to be from the earlier part of the 20th century. Still, with Sloane's credentials, it is surprising that citations to his work have not been greater.

Early American historiography on Napoleon seems totally ignored in several treatments of the subject, including the "Napoleonic Wars" entry of the *Encyclopaedia of Historians and Historical Writing* and the bibliographical essay in Geoffrey Ellis' work on Napoleon. While Sloane was the only professional historian of the five, even he is not included in the standard collections on noted American historians. [34]

It appears, that with the possible exception of Sloane (with apologies to the readability of Tarbell), the other authors remain largely relevant primarily only for Napoleonic collectors and those amateur or professional historians looking to use older materials to illustrate development of the literature. The advent of electronic sources – both online and CD – has added new access, if not relevance, to information that would otherwise be sought after by Napoleonic collectors. While these writings may only provide a faint echo from the 19th century, it is a worthy echo all the same.

20th Century
Works Citing Our Featured Authors

Alexander, R. S., *Napoleon* (New York: Oxford), 2001.

Andrews, George Gordon, *Napoleon in Review* (New York: Alfred A. Knopf), 1939.

August Fournier, *Napoleon the First: A Biography*, translated by Margaret Bacon Corwin and Arthur Dart Bissell Bourne and edited by Edward Gaylord (New York: Henry Holt and Company), 1903.

Chandler, David G., *Dictionary of the Napoleonic Wars* (New York: Macmillan Publishing Co.), 1979.

------ *The Campaigns of Napoleon* (New York: Macmillan Publishing Company), 1966.

------ (Editor-in-Chief). *Napoleon's Marshals* (New York: Macmillan Publishing Company), 1987.

Delderfield, R. F., *Imperial Sunset: The Fall of Napoleon, 1813-14* (Philadelphia: Chilton Book Company), 1968.

Dodge, Theodore Ayrault, *Napoleon*, four volumes (Boston: Houghton Mifflin Company), 1932 (original copyright 1904).

Fisher, Herbert, *Napoleon* (New York: Henry Holt and Company), 1924.

Geer, Walter, *Napoleon the First: An Intimate Biography* (New York: Brentano's), 1921.

Gottschalk, Louis R., *The Era of the French Revolution, 1715-1815* (Boston: H Houghton Mifflin), 1929.

Guerard, Albert, *Reflections on the Napoleonic Legend* (New York: Charles Scribner's), 1924.

------- *Napoleon I: A Great Life in Brief* (New York: Alfred A. Knopf), 1956.

Headley, P. C., *The Life of Napoleon Bonaparte* (New York: A.L. Burt Co.), 1903.

Markham, J., David in *Napoleon: The Final Verdict*, multiple authors with an introduction by Philip J. Haythornthwaite (London: Arms and Armour), 1996.

Macartney, Clarence Edward and Dorrance, Gordon, *The Bonapartes in America* (Philadelphia: Dorrance and Company), 1939.

Rose, J. Holland, "Napoleon: His Aims and Achievements," in *Universal World History* edited by J. A. Hammerton (New York: Wise & Co.), 1937.

3
CRAFTING THE LIFE

The paper "Crafting the Life of Napoleon: The Workshop of American Authors since 1900" was delivered at the Michigan Academy of Science, Arts & Letters, on March 20, 2009, at Wayne State University, Detroit.

"To the biographer who has done his research, who knows his subject and has settled upon the form and the shape and the plot of his book, there comes always and at last that moment when he sits alone in his room, the typewriter before him, a clean sheet of paper staring up – and no one and nothing to help him...It is an awesome moment..." – Catherine Drinker Bowen [1]

This essay examines the approach of 16 American authors in crafting the life of Napoleon. While there are thousands of books about Napoleon, that number actually becomes manageable when we limit the list to American authors, and then again to those in the form of biography, and even more so by including only those published since 1900. Ideally, the range would be restricted even further; and while the primary focus is on those who laid the foundation of the American effort in this area during the first half of the century, it seemed too incomplete to neglect recent, especially living, authors. Therefore, the final section of this paper addresses their contributions too.

The inspiration for this topic comes from the biography that remains the classic of Napoleonic biography (see Chapter 5), Emil Ludwig's (1881-1948) *Napoleon* (1926), which became the No. 2 best-selling non-fiction book in the U.S. during 1927, just behind Will Durant's *Story of Philosophy*. The unique approach of his biography – the use of present tense and the organization of the book – nicely illustrates the "art and craft" of biography. The ability to provide the reader a portrait of the subject is what this paper attempts to cover; what biographer Catherine Drinker Bowen calls "the shape of what goes into our book." [2]

While it could be argued that any treatment involving Napoleon's life could illustrate the craft of assembling biographical information, it was necessary to restrict the scope of this paper to only consider those authors who have written about his entire life, therefore excluding many interesting and valuable studies about specific aspects of his life and campaigns. During the 19th century, America had five authors whose works on Napoleon stood out, by training two ministers, an attorney, a professional historian, and a teacher turned writer: Joel T. Headley (1813-1897), John S.C. Abbott (1805-1877), John C. Ropes (1836-1899), William Milligan Sloane (1850-1928), and Ida M. Tarbell (1857-1944). While their efforts resulted in a substantial contribution to early American Napoleonic historiography, these works are appreciated by collectors, but have only produced a faint echo for historians and biographers during the 20th century and the beginning of the 21st century (see Chapter 2). It should also be noted that Sloane's monumental life saw new editions published early in the 20th century. [3]

I: RELATED GENRES
Military Career

In defining the scope of this essay, it was difficult to ignore three related genres that cover Napoleon from birth to death: his military career, the age itself, and juvenile biography. Still, these authors were crafters of Napoleon's life, and need to be included. [4]

Two accounts focusing on his military career are both by professional Army officers, Theodore Ayrault Dodge (1842-1909) and Trevor Nevitt Dupuy (1916-1995). Dodge, who lost a leg at Gettysburg and retired in 1870 as a brevet lieutenant colonel, produced a total of 12 volumes on Alexander, Hannibal, Caesar, Gustavus, Frederick, and Napoleon between 1890-1907 in his "History of the Art of War" series. The four volumes on Napoleon appeared between 1904-1907 totaling 2,721 pages. In his preface to volume 3, Dodge wrote:

"Over thirty years ago, the author began the study of Napoleon in the ample library of the late John C. Ropes of Boston, a clear-headed critic, an able writer, and an authority on the subject. This study he has continued at intervals ever since, and for the last five years in Paris; and his travels and studies in working up the campaigns of the other great captains, as they fitted into the History of the Art of War, have aided him in understanding what this last of them did...The author pretends to have made no great discoveries, but his study of the subject has been long, his travels over campaigning grounds and battlefields have occupied years, his presentation is new, the criticisms are original, and the treatment is exhaustive." [5]

Two chapters stand out: his 20-page "The Youth and the Company Officer," and his 48-page "The Man and Soldier" at the end of his study. This set of books, like Ludwig's biography, feature unique headings at the top of every page. In the chapter on Napoleon's youth, the headings include: His Parents, Mental Equipment, His Aspirations, and Attention to Duty. In the concluding paragraphs Dodge wrote:

"Out of these years only the energy, persistency and, if you like, the gambling instinct, or readiness to take chances, stand out from the other traits of the half-formed character...He had, however, shown two of the essential factors of the great captain, force of intellect and force of character. Would the third factor, opportunity, ever come?" [6]

In his second-to-last chapter, Dodge wrote "...and now we have to gauge his character; and what is told of the man is only to throw light upon the captain." [7] Page headings for this chapter include Personal Appearance, Moral Courage, Capacity for Work, Born to Command, Genius and Power to Create, Arrogance Grows Fast, Juggling with Facts, Hunger for Approval, The Emperor's Office, Misrepresentation of Facts, Saturated with Selfishness, and Qualities of a Leader.

Colonel Dupuy (West Point, class of 1938), who wrote 12 volumes in his "Military Lives" series, wrote his brief military biography (221 pages) of Napoleon in 1969, based on a textbook he had privately printed in the mid-1950s while teaching a class on American Military History. He appreciated the value of Dodge's work (specifically mentioning the 40-page chapter previously discussed) and Count Yorck von Wartenburg's *Napoleon as a General*, but wanted something shorter to serve as an introduction on the origins of modern warfare. He wrote in his foreword that, "It was, and is, my belief that the greatest single influence on modern American military doctrine was that of Napoleon." [8]

Age of Napoleon

This genre includes J. Christopher Herold's *Age of Napoleon* (1963) and Will and Ariel Durant's *Age of Napoleon* (1975). Herold (1919-1964), born in Czechoslovakia and later becoming an American citizen, was editor of the Columbia University Press and the Stanford University Press. The author of four other Napoleonic titles, he wrapped this story of Napoleon around the age itself, including details of political, cultural, military, economic, and social aspects of the period telling about the age (and there is even more detail about the age of Napoleon in the beautifully illustrated Horizon edition). The organization of the book follows Napoleon's entire life and the final chapter, "Legacy and Legend," is especially powerful. [9]

The Durant book was the final volume in their famous *Story of Civilization*, which they wrote from 1935-1975, and earned their publisher, Simon and Schuster, the Carey Thomas Award for creative publishing and the Durants the Presidential Medal of Freedom (The Durant's *Rousseau and Revolution*, the volume preceding Napoleon, won the Pulitzer Prize). Will Durant (1885-1981) earned his doctorate from Columbia University in 1917 and was able to begin five decades of practicing "integral" history thanks to the success of his *The Story of Philosophy* at the age of 41. His wife Ariel (1898-1981) assisted him in his work of integral history and they finally added her as an author for the final volumes, including the one on Napoleon. Their 1,800 typed pages on Napoleon turned into 872 printed pages appeared in 1975 and was made a Book-of-the-Month selection for January 1976, "winning for us an added audience of 100,000 readers, recalls Will Durant." [10]

"And shall we confess it," write the Durants in their preface, "we had nurtured from our adolescence a sly, fond interest in Napoleon as no mere warmonger and despot, but as also a philosopher seldom deceived by pretense and as a psychologist who had ceaselessly studied human nature in the mass and in individual men." They spent five years on the book, working with materials they had assembled for 60 years. [11] Mentioning the 200,000 books on Napoleon, Ariel posed the question in their memoirs, "What could we add to that embarrassment of riches except some new order and synthesis?" [12]

The work is divided into five books, including a 21-page chapter on "Napoleon Himself" focusing on Body, Mind, Character, The General, The Ruler, The Philosopher, and What Was He? At the end of their work, they wrote:

> "Recovering from him, we too, authors and readers, fulfill his prediction – that the world would greet his death with an exhalation of relief. He was an exhausting force, a phenomenon of energy contained and explosive, a rising, burning, waning flame that consumed those who touched him intimately. We have not found in history another soul that burned so intensely and so long...He remains the outstanding figure of his time, with something noble about him that survives despite his selfishness in power and his occasional descents from grandeur in defeat." [13]

Juvenile/Young Adult Biography

Those of us who are currently in our fifties or older – and long-time fans of biography – may be familiar with *Napoleon and the Battle of Waterloo* (1953) by Frances Winwar, one of the many Landmark books on biography and history popular with elementary students. The title notwithstanding, this is a biography of Napoleon. The 183-page book features 17 chapters such as: The Corsican Boy, The Young Lieutenant, Revolution, Coronation at Notre Dame, The Snows of Russia, and Waterloo. Winwar begins by describing Napoleon's homeland – Corsica, the rocky island in the Mediterranean – and completes the book with a chapter titled, "The Carriage at Bullock's," referring to Bullock's Museum in London where Napoleon's carriage ended up after Waterloo. This chapter describes Napoleon's final days on St. Helena:

"Napoleon, however, left behind him a legend and a moral lesson. He showed what a man can accomplish through strength of purpose, courage, and imagination. He destroyed the last remnants of feudalism in Europe and abolished the Inquisition in Spain. He helped to build the modern code of laws. He encouraged art and science and education. But once he gained power he paired it with his colossal ambition. The two, like fiery steeds driven recklessly for his own glory, plunged him and his empire to destruction. So great was his fall at Waterloo that since then all defeat has been known by its name." [14]

Manfred Weidhorn was born in Austria and moved to Brooklyn, New York, in 1941 at age ten, eventually earning his doctorate at Columbia College. Atheneum brought out his 212-page *Napoleon* in 1986 for young adults. He introduces his topic with the familiar story about the book by British Archbishop Whately, *Historic Doubts Relative to Napoleon Bonaparte* (1819) to make the point that people should be able to believe in stories of the Bible, since common sense would lead someone to believe that a life as extraordinary as Napoleon's could also not possibly be true. "This obscure but amusing volume establishes, more than does almost anything else, that Napoleon led one of the most exciting and legendary of all lives. Here is the story of that life." For this audience, the author explained that he read half a dozen of the major and standard works, choosing not to do original research, having "neither the time, nor the expertise, nor the necessity to do so." [15]

Albert Marrin, born in 1936 and still producing biographies, is the author of more than two dozen books for young readers, and wrote *Napoleon and the Napoleonic Wars* in 1991 for young adults (ages 12 and up). Marrin, a former colleague of Weidhorns (and who gave Weidhorn the idea of writing young adult books) begins with a prologue about Napoleon's coronation in 1804, followed by eight chapters detailing his life: A Born Soldier, The Little Corporal, Emperor of the Republic, England's Floating Fortresses, Master of Europe, Russia 1812, The Road to Waterloo, and Eagle on the Rock.

Marrin relates to his young readers by telling them how the Bonaparte's house in Ajaccio on Corsica can still be visited today, and how Napoleon's school Ecole Militaire de Paris translates as Paris Military School, was located near where the Eiffel Tower stands today. Marrin writes in his prologue that, "So long as people fight wars, the name of Napoleon will be honored by those who follow the soldier's profession. Our job must be to understand the man, setting him in his own time." As one review mentioned, the text is readable, dramatic, and well-documented...and the author does not shy away from grim realities" (as demonstrated in his account of the retreat from Moscow). [16]

II
THE FOUNDATION - WATSON TO GUERARD

The beginning decades of the 20th century are rich with American Napoleonic biographies, with five works discussed here. In 1902, Dodd, Mead and Company brought out *Napoleon: A Sketch of His Life, Character, Struggles, and Achievements* by Thomas E. Watson (1856-1922). Writing his preface on December 24, 1901, from Thomson, Georgia, Watson – an attorney, politician, and author of *The Story of France* (1898) and *Life of Thomas Jefferson* (1900) – explained that he:

> "Has made the effort to portray Napoleon as he appears to an average man. Archives have not been rummaged, new sources of information have not been discovered; the author merely claims to have used such authorities, old and new, as are accessible to any diligent student. No attempt has been made to give a full and detailed account of Napoleon's life or work. To do so would have required the labor of a decade, and the result would be almost a library. The author has tried to give to the great Corsican his proper historical position, his true rating as a man and a rule, -- together with a just estimate of his achievements." [17]

Contrary to his preface, Watson's 719 pages do present as full an account as possible in one volume, through 49 chapters. The first three chapters are, Corsica, Boyhood, and Lieutenant, and half-way through is a 25-page chapter on "Habits and Characteristics," with a

24 line description of his eyes and gaze: "All accounts agree that his glance was uncomfortably fierce and penetrating; or, at other times, intolerably fierce and intimidating; or, again, irresistibly soft, tender, magnetic." Watson uses this chapter to discuss Napoleon's voice, appearance, temperament, curiosity, tastes, work style, how he related to people, and how "his natural instinct was to make improvements." [18]

George W. Jacobs & Company of Philadelphia published *Napoleon and the End of the French Revolution* by Charles F. Warwick in 1910. The 481-page volume was a sequel to his three books that combine biography and the French Revolution. The title is misleading, because this volume is a biography, much different from works such as Gershoy's. In his preface, Warwick thanks William J. Latta of Philadelphia for the engravings and etchings, many being original sketches made by artists contemporary with Napoleon, and never before published. Following chapter 31 on St. Helena and his death are two chapters are simply titled "Napoleon Bonaparte," with these combined 19 pages serving as a conclusion about his life. "It is hard to delineate truthfully, accurately, the character of Napoleon," Warwick writes. He addresses his Napoleon's versatility, his relations with his troops, as a public administrator (how he spent much more time in Paris vs. campaigning than people assume), and how, while "No one thinks of classing him with Washington and Lincoln; but considering him from a purely intellectual standpoint as an original and a constructive genius, as a soldier and a civil administrator, he has not in the history of the world had his equal." [19]

James Morgan, author of biographies of Lincoln and Theodore Roosevelt, wrote *In the Footsteps of Napoleon: His Life and its Famous Scenes*, published by Macmillan in 1915. Morgan and his wife traveled nearly 20,000 miles for his research "to see and portray the man in his various backgrounds, to bring closer his habitations and battlefields, to simplify the geography of his campaigns." The beginning of his travels coincided with the beginnings of Waterloo centennial planning, and as he notes, the War of Nations (WWI) had already begun. In his foreword to the 524-page book, he writes:

"I have tried to present him simply as a man of the people who, in a period of chaos, as called out of the crowd to embody and vindicate the race of common men against the privileged few, to sweep away ancient systems and wrongs, and, as the incarnation of the Great Revolution, to be enthroned about monarchs of long descent. In short, I have represented him as the servant of a mighty power not of himself *that o'er him planned* (Morgan's emphasis) and which, with the pitilessness of nature, cast him away when, blinded by personal ambition, he was no longer faithful and useful to its purpose. This is the Napoleon, who, after the lapse of a century, retains his dominion over the imagination of the world, supreme in the admiration and the disappointment, in the applause and reproach of men." [20]

Morgan's 53 chapters follow a traditional approach, concluding with the chapter "Across a Century," where he discusses Napoleon's tomb, a review of his life, and comments that had Napoleon "only seen and welcomed the dawning of this age of democracy, he would be its prophet, and the Invalides would be more than a brilliant spectacle; it would be the shrine of mankind." [21] A five-page chronology completes the work.

Walter Geer (1857-1937) is our most prolific author during this period, with Brentano's publishing his *Napoleon the First: An Intimate Biography* in 1921 selling for $5, followed by uniform editions of *Napoleon and Josephine: The Rise of the Empire* (1924), *Napoleon and Marie-Louise: The Fall of the Empire* (1925), and three volumes of *Napoleon and His Family: The Story of a Corsican Clan* (1927-1929). Writing his foreword to *Napoleon the First* from New York City in May, 1921, the Massachusetts native and graduate of Williams College and National University said of books on Napoleon, "there are comparatively few which give an unprejudiced picture of the man. For the most part no judgment has been passed upon him but that either of profound antipathy or of blind admiration." With the passing of 100 years since his death, "we think that the time has come for a more impartial estimate...Let us then endeavor to depict Napoleon as he was, and 'nothing extenuate, nor set down aught in malice.' [22]

His 390-page *Napoleon the First* is presented in 23 chapters, with the final one focusing on his personality. "A century has not been long enough to arrive at a conclusion as to the full meaning of his life; nor has it produced any man comparable to him in force of will, energy, or in sheer power of intellect," he writes at the beginning of the 12 pages, followed by commentary on the following topics: influence on Europe, social equality, political liberty, higher education, publicity, personal appearance, health, method of work, dictating and writing, mental equipment, family relations, career, physical and moral courage, statesmanship, moral, imagination, ambition, lack of organization, leadership, and comparison to Caesar. [23]

While this one volume best fits our parameters for this paper, it is difficult to ignore his other volumes since, as a set, they encompass a full-ranging biography. Writing in the foreword of the first volume of the *Napoleon and His Family* trilogy, Geer says:

"It is impossible to understand fully the drama of the life of Napoleon without taking into consideration two factors, practically ignored by historians, which had a decisive bearing upon his career: his physical heritage [meaning his health], and the influence of his family," adding that this is the story of the family "as it influenced his design, his acts, and his destiny." [24]

It is interesting how he framed the lives of Napoleon's two wives. Introducing his *Napoleon and Josephine*, Geer wrote that, "The aversion which many feel towards Napoleon is not a little due to what they conceive to be the cruelty with which he treated the woman who for fourteen years was the companion of his glory," continuing that the author "holds no brief either for the prosecution for the defense. He wants to draw a portrait – not to pronounce a judgment: his object is to depict Josephine as she was, and he leaves the reader to decide as to her goodness." [25]

Meanwhile, introducing his work *Napoleon and Marie-Louise*, Geer wrote that, "Except as the consort of Napoleon, Marie-Louise has no historical interest, and it is only in her relations with him that she will be considered. Our theme is the Austrian marriage and its effect on the Russian alliance: these two events determined the fate of Napoleon." [26]

Albert Guerard (1880-1959) was born in Paris, educated in Paris and London, and moved to the U.S. at the age of 26, teaching at a number of colleges including Rice Institute and Stanford University. His *Reflections on the Napoleonic Legend* (1924) is a masterpiece, but it is his *Napoleon I* (1956) in Knopf's 'Great Lives in Brief' series that is our focus. This 199-page biography is the best short biography produced by an American writer; our version of England's brief works of art by H.A.L. Fisher (1912), and Herbert Butterfield (1956). "This will be the story of a *human* life," he wrote in his foreword. "Of the multitudinous writings about Napoleon...many place him beyond our common humanity...After fifty years of study, Napoleon appears to me as neither angel nor beast, but as human, all too human." The present book, he explains, "is pure biography," noting that he addressed the 'Legend' in his 1924 work. [27]

Guerard's story is told in 11 chapters: Young Bonaparte, General Bonaparte: Rehearsals for Empire: Italy and Egypt, The Man of the Hour (First Consul), The Parting of the Ways (Consul for Life), Napoleon Emperor: The Ascending Star (1804-1807), Dark Omens (1808-1809), Splendors and Miseries (1810-1811), Downfall: The Russian Campaign, The German and the French Campaigns (1813-1814), Elba and the Hundred Days, and Epilogue: St. Helena and Paris. "If we seek biography, not hagiography," he wrote in his epilogue, "the story of a great life as it was actually lived, if we strive to understand Napoleon the human being, then we must bear in mind that Napoleon the Demigod was conceived in St. Helena, came of age in 1830, and was solemnly canonized in 1840." [28]

III
RECENT SCHOLARSHIP: SCHOM TO ENGLUND

It seems odd that with all the books on Napoleon, we have a gap in American biography production on Napoleon from Guerard to Alan Schom, whose 888-page work appeared in 1998. Schom, one of four historians featured in this section and author of two other Napoleonic works (on the Waterloo campaign and Trafalgar), wrote this biography because Napoleon "badly needed to be dealt with fully and properly in one volume covering every aspect of his life and character, employing all the new research and archival documents."

Like Morgan, he attempted to retrace Napoleon's footsteps, writing in his preface that, "It has been a long, arduous, but fascinating odyssey requiring almost every minute of every day," going on to say that, "I have reexamined his many military campaigns, his treatment of those countries and peoples he conquered, his relations with colleagues and subordinates, and his ideas, motives, and performance."

Finally, he wrote that, "My goal is to provide a balanced insight into Napoleon and his actions." Schom spent ten years researching and writing his 41 chapters, each one beginning with a quote by Napoleon. The biography seems to end abruptly with Napoleon's death, weighing in on the cause of his death: "there is no doubt that Napoleon was murdered," pointing to one of Napoleon's aides in exile, Charles Tristan de Montholon. In the epilogue, instead of going with any discussion of legend or legacy, he recounts the horrors Europe endured at Napoleon's hands and states that Napoleon's impact on the emerging German nationalism later in the century resulting in Prussia's subsequent victory of France. "I have attempted to give Napoleon Bonaparte his rightful due," he wrote. [29]

The military historian Robert Asprey brought out two books during 2000 and 2001, *The Rise of Napoleon Bonaparte* followed by the *Reign of Napoleon Bonaparte*, with the two volumes totaling 1,060 pages (580 and 480 pages respectively). His chapters are short, but are numerous with 48 and 35 respectively in the two books. Each chapter begins with a quotation with notes appearing at the end of each. The first volume begins with a four-page piece simply titled "In the Beginning" about Corsica fighting for and losing their bid for independence from the French before Napoleon's birth and ends with Austerlitz in 1805. It is interesting that his second volume was published in the United Kingdom as *The Rise and Fall of Napoleon Bonaparte: Volume Two*.

In his "A Note to the Reader," Asprey – a former Marine captain and veteran of two wars – wrote that, "Ever since his untimely death at the age of 51 on the forlorn island of St. Helena in 1821, Napoleon Bonaparte has too often been the victim of biographical and historical exuberance, of unhealthy literary passions that treat him either as demi-god (mainly French authors) or as devil incarnate (mainly British authors)," adding his displeasure with recently published biographies. He continued:

> "Napoleon's relatively short life is a story of massive successes and disastrous failures, intense loves and violent hatreds, genius and stupidity, vision and cupidity, arrogance and ignorance, intrigue and treachery, short-term satisfactions and long-term frustrations – of unfettered power once intended for the public good but in time diluted by overweening ambition and conceit...Napoleon was a sum of his parts which is why I have treated him, warts and all, as a human being, as child, student, man, soldier, general, lover, husband, father, ruler, emperor, conqueror and statesman. His story is an intensely dramatic saga, presented in terms not of our day but of his..." [30]

Historian J. David Markham published his biography *Napoleon's Road to Glory: Triumphs, Defeats and Immortality* in 2003, illustrated entirely from his collection of Napoleonic snuffboxes, prints, and small decorative arts. His *Road to Glory* is 320 pages divided into an introduction and prologue followed by six parts, completed by an epilogue. Writing from Olympia, Washington, Markham introduced the work with a question followed by a commentary of Napoleon's rise and fall:

> "How was it that a minor nobleman from Corsica, who was no better than middle class in France, could rise to become Napoleon I, Emperor of the French and so dominate Europe? What led him to those heights? Just as importantly, what caused him to fall, rise again, and then fall to lonely exile on an isolated rock of an island? This book will help provide answers to these questions." [31]

We then find the prologue covering Napoleon's early life and education followed by the parts: The Soldier and the Revolution, The Years as Consul, A Republican Emperor, Steps Towards the End, The Final Collapse and Saint Helena and Immortality. The epilogue features: The Eagle Returns: The Final Road to Glory. Each part has from four to 12 chapters and notes follow the end of each chapter.

Two years later, his *Napoleon for Dummies* appeared, what has to be the most fun, yet still thoroughly informative, Napoleon biography ever published. *Napoleon for Dummies* is 364 pages of pure creativity, light-hearted, but still authoritive, complete with a "cheat sheet" that tears out covering his military career and legacy. There are six parts, each with three to six chapters: Beginnings (beginning with "Why Remember Napoleon?"), Building an Empire, Losing an Empire, A True Revolutionary, Influencing Nations: Diplomacy and Legacy, and The Part of Tens (10 most interesting battlefields to visit, 10 pieces of advice for Napoleon, and 10-plus best sources for further information).

In his introduction, he explained that his book tries to "give you a chance to get to know Napoleon the man." The first three parts present a chronological look, followed by parts detailing more of his life and times: "...that are better dealt with by themselves, rather than squished into a chronological table." As with Road to Glory, all the illustrations come from his private collection. There are a lot of moving parts to the volume, as with all of the Dummies series, such as side-bar information featured in shaded boxes, and icons accompanying the text alerting readers to information worth remembering, identifying technical information, and text focusing on his legend. [32]

Steven Englund wrote *Napoleon: A Political Life* in 2004, a 575-page biography – a full biography regardless of the title. The Distinguished New York University Professor at the American University of Paris divides his work into four books, each with three to four chapters (each beginning with a quote), and each containing from three to nine sub-sections. The book opens with the two-page section "Frisson," discussing the impact of Napoleon's tomb. "Visiting Les Invalides is like visiting the Lincoln Memorial: amid all the funeral marble and the airless geometric space, *something is alive.*" But at Napoleon's Tomb, says Englund, "something is different. Here the abyss peers back." At the end of "Frisson," he writes of the "Sphinx-like qualities of good and evil and mystery. Most present in this place is the awe-evoking sense of human *possibility*, which is a different thing from hope." [33]

Coming at the end of his book is his reflective "Introduction (Misplaced): This Author, This Book," a wonderful six-page essay which could stand on its own in a future anthology of Napoleonic scholarship. "For better or for worse, this is a *political* life, not a military, or an intimate life of its subject. For what it is worth, Napoleon would have approved such an approach, if certainly not most of my interpretations or conclusions," Englund wrote. He explains how he considered using "The Empire of Circumstance" as the book's sub-title, "so great was the power of the French Revolution in determining Napoleon's rise and his enduring attainments." He concludes that he hoped "…to convey to the reader our 'tremble' before Napoleon – in fear and disapproval, but also in admiration and, at bottom, perhaps even in fear of our own longing for him…" [34]

According to Englund:

"…a life of Napoleon Bonaparte is an unnerving undertaking, and the problem in recent decades has lain in getting serious biographers to take a serious shot at a life of this man." Englund gives credit to historian David Bell, who "shook his fist at the over-sized figure of Napoleon who has intimidated and repulsed us for too long." Englund says that "Would-be biographers confront a great problem beyond the superabundance of sources – far too much for one person to read, let along master – and that is the infamous un-graspability of the subject." [35]

Englund does not believe that Americans have played a very key role in Napoleonic studies:

"Napoleonic biography escapes many (most), not merely Americans. He is, as it happens, one of the hardest characters to search out in a bio, because…History takes over where the writer and reader were hoping for biography. American scholars need to have an extraordinarily deep and broad sense of things European (not just French), in order to write revealingly about Napoleon, and that takes more than just sitting in a library or archives" [36]

David Bell believes that recent American biographies have been written by amateurs, mostly aficionados of military history, and tend to highlight Napoleon's qualities of military leadership. "They have generally underplayed Napoleon's role as a builder of the modern French state, and as an inheritor of the French Revolution. They are often written with distressing ignorance of broader European history of the period, and of the work of French Napoleon experts." [37]

American historians such as Englund and Bell (and Australian Philip Dwyer) continue breaking new ground in how we study Napoleon.

4
THE PUBLISHERS

The paper "The Lives of Napoleon: American Publishing, 1821-1921" was delivered at the Michigan Academy of Science, Arts & Letters on March 2, 2012, at Alma College.

> "The publisher must be a businessman. Yet, in essence, book publishing is also a profession and one of the creative arts. The good publisher does not merely accept a book from an author, dress it in suitable attire, and present it to the world; he creates books out of his own vision of markets and therein lies much of the attraction to the man of active imagination."
> – E. M. Crane [1]

While the study of Napoleon includes thousands of books – which naturally attracts attention to the authors – an area lacking attention are the publishers of these books. The purpose of this paper is to provide a survey of American publishers during the 100 years following his death in 1821. Instead of following the publication of his story by author or chronologically by publication date, I've decided to organize this survey geographically, focusing on a variety of "publication events" at each publisher.

Selecting the first 100 years is arbitrary – the first 50 years would provide plenty of examples of this topic in American publishing – but useful incorporating the centennials of his birth in 1869, the battle of Waterloo in 1915, and his death in 1921. Deciding which publishers and titles to pursue is also arbitrary, beginning with my personal collection, surveying available books online (Advanced Book Exchange includes 101 books as first editions for our dates), and including research on American publishing houses. Although this survey is restricted to American publishers, we will survey the works of authors regardless of nationality.

Some interesting nuances of these years in American publishing include: competition from English publishers, the size of editions (a press run of 750 to 1,000 was the standard), books were very often a work of art (decorative spines and covers, tissue protecting illustrative plates, gilded edges, heavy paper stock, and advertising for the publisher), costs for books were high for the time, although prices dropped with printing advances (early on, titles ranged from 50 cents to $1.25 for one volume to $3 for multi volumes), rampant copyright infringement, the early connection in the industry of publishing, importing, and bookselling, and the ever-changing landscape of publishers, including frequent name changes and mergers. Not to mention, the frequent lack of publication dates, and sometimes the lack of the identification of the author. [2]

Not only were early press runs modest, but during the 1830s to early 1840s, only about 100 books total were issued annually by American publishers. With the mass distribution of books by the mid-1850s, however, the American publishing industry was valued at $16 million, which included producing more school books than all of Europe's publishers combined. [3]

Interest in Napoleon (along with other military history topics) was stimulated by the Mexican War (1846-1848) by both military professionals and the general public. "The lists of all publishers reflected this public demand, and items of Napoleonana and Fredericana (Frederick the Great) appeared in endless profusion," wrote the president of a New York publishing house in a company history. [4]

By 1909, publishers were beginning to focus on publishing and selling their own titles, and closing their retail stores. The publishing trends we will observe in general speak to the power of the effectiveness of efforts toward wide-spread public education in our young nation, and in respects to Napoleon, to his wide presence in American popular culture.

Philadelphia

Our story begins in Philadelphia, which was not only the largest city in the nation at the beginning of the nineteenth century (with a population of 70,000), but was for a time the publishing center of the United States. [5] We will look at five key publishers for this city.

Our nation's first big publishing event regarding the life of Napoleon occurred in 1827 at the publishing house of Carey, Lea & Carey, situated on Chestnut Street. The house, publisher of *The American Quarterly Review*, *The Philadelphia Journal of the Medical and Physical Sciences*, and the American publisher of the English *Common Law Review*, had what historian John Tebbel calls "a momentous year." In addition to a change in the name of the firm – adding on another Carey brother – the firm brought out a three-volume set of books "eagerly awaited by the public," writes historian John Tebbel, Sir Walter Scott's *The Life of Napoleon Buonaparte*.

While copyright infringement was typical during this century (law in 1891), Carey, Lea & Carey actually negotiated with the author of the Waverley novels before he had finished the manuscript, paying $1,475 for the American rights. According to Tebbel, this was "a record sale for a foreign author at a time when few of them got anything at all." Published in an edition of 12,250, "extremely large for the time," the firm invested $20,000 in the book, but cleared more than $13,000. This edition of Scott's biography of Napoleon, the final writing project by the famous Scottish author, was one of only 52 titles brought out that year in America. [6]

The set, featuring ragged pages along the bottom and side with paper of varying sizes and thickness, contains 1,283 pages, each volume totaling 516, 399, and 368 pages respectively. Credited with the stereotype of the book is J. Howe. The book is bound in plain blue boards, which the purchaser could have custom bound (there are first American editions available for sale today that reference leather binding). An announcement facing the title page warns the reader of several errors in the paging and heads of chapters "in consequence of irregularity in the receipt of the copy from England." Also, an appendix in the third volume has an errata consisting of two pages, correcting information by page number. The binding title of the book, with glued paper labels, is *Life if Napoleon* by the Author of Waverly. The publisher has advertisements for its journals and books at the beginning of the second and third volumes.

The firm's next large Napoleon event was in 1832 with the publication of Bourrienne's memoirs *Life of Napoleon Bonaparte*. And then in 1838, when – as E. L. Carey & A. Hart – they published *Napoleon and His Times* by Caulincourt (Duke of Vicenza) in two volumes, totaling 483 pages (253 and 230 respectively), listing T.K. & P.G. Collins as the printers. This set featured ads in front of each volume, and was bound in decorative red boards with tan title labels pasted on the spine. Ten years later, the firm (then Carey & Hart), published *The Life of Napoleon Bonaparte* by the English author William Hazlitt. [7] The three-volume set went for $3.

The next most prolific Philadelphia publisher on Napoleon was Henry T. Coates & Co., also located on Chestnut Street, using the symbol PC. Coates was a publisher of Sir Walter Scott's Waverly novels in a "Household" edition of 23 volumes at $1 each. This house issued four different titles of significance during the 1800s, although the dates of publication are difficult to confirm. *Life and Campaigns of Napoleon Bonaparte* by M.A. Arnault and C.L.F. Panckoucke (translated from the French), was issued in a "new edition, illustrated" in an Alta edition two volumes in one totaling 498 pages with a binding title of "Life of Napoleon," but with the title "Memoirs of Napoleon Bonaparte" as the section titles for both "books," 247 and 251 pages respectively.

The house published three notable titles under the name Porter & Coates, which included another edition of the Arnault and Panckoucke book (my copy has a inscription dated 1880 as an award, which leads me to think this edition was new that year). The page design has the text inside a box. Illustrated with black and white plates, *The Life of Napoleon Bonaparte: Emperor of France* by John Gibson Lockhart (1794-1854, the son-in-law of Sir Walter Scott), featured a decorative cover with unique page headings on all right-hand pages accompanied by the years being discussed. The introduction to the 392 page book refers to the volume as an abridgment of Lockhart's life of Napoleon. Bearing a copyright of 1854 by H.C. Peck & Theo. Bliss (but my copy published during or after the Civil War, since this edition includes an ad for a book on the Civil War) *The Camp-Fires of Napoleon: Comprising the most brilliant achievements of the Emperor and his Marshals* by Henry C. Watson was published as an Alta edition. The 448-page book contains 16 pages of ads in the back for other titles from Porter & Coates, and this edition appears to be for younger readers.

John E. Potter and Company, situated on Sansom Street, published numerous biographies at $1.75 each. *Napoleon and His Campaigns: His Army and his Generals* has no author or date listed, however my copy is inscribed with 1882, and the preface cites the volume as a "compilation" of the works of Scott, Lockhart, Clarke and other English authors. The 422-page book sports a decorative cover with a binding title of *Napoleon and His Campaigns*. Other Napoleon titles mentioned in the book's ads included *Corsica and the Early Life of Napoleon*, translated by the Hon. E. Joy Morris and *Historical and Secret Memoirs of the Empress Josephine*, translated from the French of M'lle Le Normand by Jacob M. Howman. Toward the end of the period we are examining, they published *Corsica: Picturesque, Historical and Social with a Sketch of the Early Life of Napoleon* by Edward Joy Morris in 1920.

Other publishers of this city of note include G. D. Miller's 1855 edition of William Hazlitt's *The Life of Napoleon Bonaparte* (three volumes in one) in full-leather with marbled edges. Also, J.B. Lippincott Co. published several editions of Hazlitt, one in 1875 in leather with marbled boards and gilt on the top edges as a multi-volume set and again in 1878 in three-volumes with tissue protecting an illustration, a decorative "N" on the cover, and a gilt image of Napoleon on the spine.

The John C. Winston Company brought out two volumes by the English author Norwood Young in 1914 and 1915, *Napoleon in Exile*, with one volume on Elba and the other on St. Helena, timed with the 100th anniversary of Napoleon's two abdications. Those two volumes were printed by William Brendon and Son, LTD, printers, Plymouth, with numerous illustrations and decorative covers. [8]

New York City

Our survey of this location includes 19 publishing houses. The first major Napoleonic publishing event for New York was in 1846, at the recently established Baker and Scribner, with their shop at the Brick Church Chapel on Park Row and Nassau Street. They enjoyed an early "lucky success" when Joel Tyler Headley came into their establishment with a just-completed manuscript. Their publication of *Napoleon and His Marshals*, a two-volume set selling for $2.50, becoming a long-time best-seller.

"This book was instantly popular," says Tebbel, partly due to public interest in military matters because of the new war with Mexico. This set was on Baker and Scribner's first "list" and was possibly their first book. *Napoleon and His Marshals* was printed with decorative boards, even edges, gold gilt for the spine title, and tissues protecting the 12 plates. The set totaled 647 pages (331 and 316 respectively). The 1847 edition in my possession is already identified as the 10th edition. The 10th edition contains ads for other books for sale at their shop, along with excerpts of reviews. [9] Later, as Charles Scribner's Sons, the publishing house kept the set in print (one of these printings was in 1861). Baker and Scribner also published Headley's next two books – *Washington and His Generals* and *The Sacred Mountain* – with these three titles combined selling 200,000 copies in the first two years, and eventually 500,000 copies collectively. [10]

The next major event was Harper & Brothers, established in 1817, and the largest, oldest, and most influential New York house of the nineteenth century. According to historian Hellmut Lehmann-Haupt, Harpers was "one of the most successful publishers in the world" by the time of our Civil War. In 1855 they brought out John S.C. Abbott's *The History of Napoleon Bonaparte*, followed by a "new edition" in 1883. The two-volume set totaled 1,277 pages (611 and 666 respectively) with numerous hundreds of black and white sketches by C. E. Doepler and maps by Jacob Wells. The binding title is *The Life of Napoleon Bonaparte* and is on labels, on blue boards. Their 1855-1858 price for this set was $5 and another title by Abbott (*Napoleon at St. Helena*) was listed at $2.50. [11]

Other Harper titles of note included editions of Lockhart's biography of Napoleon in two volumes for 90 cents (between 1820-1853), the 1853 publication of *History of the Captivity of Napoleon at St. Helena* by William Forsyth at $1.75 for the two-volume set, and the interesting little book, *Mr. Bonaparte of Corsica* by John Kendrick Bangs, illustrated by H. W. McVicar in 1895 (a critical commentary on Napoleon), and the classic by English historian Lord Rosebery, *Napoleon: The Last Phase* in 1900, with reprints following.

Thomas Y. Crowell & Company's *Memoirs of Napoleon Bonaparte* by Bourrienne in 1885 (edited by Col. R. W. Phipps, new and revised) in leather, with gilt edges and unique page headings (four books in two volumes). In 1914 they would bring out William Henry Hudson's *The Man Napoleon* (with tissue) and in 1915 Harold F. B. Wheeler's *The Story of Napoleon*, with the binding title *The Boy's Napoleon* (listing that it was printed by Turnbull & Spears in Edinburgh).

Leavitt & Allen Bros., located on Howard Street in New York, came out with a decorative, but undated, 422-page *Napoleon: His Army and His Generals: Their Unexampled Military Career* (with the title *Napoleon and His Army, Illustrated*, on the spine and cover, but no author mentioned), while the title page says By An American, with the preface referring to a "compiler." The cost was $1.25.

C.M. Saxton, Barker & Co., on Park Row, published an edition of Lockhart's *Life of Napoleon* – a new edition, revised and corrected – in 1860 (bearing the original copyright as 1851). The book features unique page headings and tissue.

The S.S. McClure Co., on 25th Street, published a book version of Ida M. Tarbell's *Short Life of Napoleon* in 1896, with 250 illustrations from the collection of Gardiner G. Hubbard.

The F.M. Lupton Publishing Company was the publisher of the successful (and still sought-after) series for young readers by G. A. Henty (1832-1902), several featuring Napoleonic topics, such as *One of the 28th: A Tale of Waterloo*, selling for 50 cents.

G. P. Putman's Sons, with printing by its Knickerbocker Press, published *The Personality of Napoleon* (1912) by British author J. Holland Rose (from that year's Lowell Lectures), with four pages of advertisements.

D. Appleton & Company was the publisher of the novels of Louisa Muhlbach, several of which featured Napoleonic characters, with millions of copies being sold. This house became the first American publisher of *Alice in Wonderland*.

Robert Carter & Brothers brought out an interesting little volume in 1856, *Historic Doubts Relative to Napoleon Bonaparte*.

A.L. Burt Company published Burt's Home Library, "popular literature for the masses…at a popular price" (with gilt tops at $1 each). Their collection included the *Life of Josephine* by Frederick A. Ober and J.T. Headley's *Napoleon and His Marshals*. Editions of Headley's set came out in 1900 and 1918.

The Macmillan Company, located on Fifth Avenue, came out with *In The Footsteps of Napoleon* by James Morgan in 1915, with a decorative cover, and five pages of ads of books selling for $1.50 and $2.

E.P. Dutton & Co., came out with a version of Lockhart's biography in the "Everyman's Library Series" in 1907.

A.L. Fowle came out with an edition of Lockhart's biography in 1900 as a two-volume set.

Mitchell Kennerley brought out an interesting little 89 page book in 1909 by Edward L. Andrews titled *Napoleon and America: An Outline of the relations of the United States to the Career and Downfall of Napoleon Bonaparte* (very rare, but easily available as a reprint via print-on-demand publishers; check out Advanced Book Exchange at abe.com).

R. H. Russell published a play about Napoleon II in 1900, *L'Aiglon*, by Edmond Rostand, translated by Louis N. Parker.

Derby and Miller, located in Auburn, New York, published editions of Lockhart's biography in 1851 and 1853, and then again – as Miller, Orton & Mulligan – in 1854 and in 1856.

The biggest publishing event of the nineteenth century for any publisher was the four-volume *Life of Napoleon Bonaparte* by The Century Company, written by Napoleonic scholar William Milligan Sloane. The book, initially issued through the *Century Magazine*, came out in 1896 in a large-size red leather-bound edition totaling 1,149 pages (283, 283, 270 and 313 respectively) with a total of 293 color and black and white plates. The paper was thick, the font large, with gilded top edges. The binding title was *Napoleon Bonaparte, A History*. The DeVinne Press served as the printer for this volume.

Century brought out a library edition in 1910 (revised and enlarged), also in four volumes, not decorative, but with tissue protecting the plates, totaling 1,876 pages (457, 467, 425, and 527 respectively), with 46 black and white illustrations and maps. In the preface to this edition, Professor Sloane writes, "Judging from the sales, it has been read by many tens if not hundreds of thousands of readers…Throughout these fourteen years the demand has been very large and steady, considering the size and cost of the volumes." [12]

And finally, in New York at the end of the scope of our survey – the 100th year anniversary of Napoleon's death – was Brentano's publication of the first of a series of Napoleonic studies by New York-based historian Walter Geer, with *Napoleon the First: An Intimate Biography* issued in 1921 (printed by the Plimpton Press of Norwood, Massachusetts).

The 390-page book – with tissue only on the plate facing the title page, decorative binding, gilded top edges and rough edges on the side – was followed throughout the 1920s by five other titles (two volumes, *Napoleon and Josephine: The Rise of the Empire*, 1924, and *Napoleon and Marie-Louise: The Fall of the Empire*, 1925; followed by three volumes of *Napoleon and His Family: The Story of A Corsican*, 1927-1929. [13]

Brentano's also brought out an interesting little book in 1900 about Napoleon II, *The Romance of L'Aiglon*, the authorized translation from the French of Carolus by J. Paul Wilson. The 156-page book was printed at the press of J. J. Little & Co., Astor Place, New York.

Boston, Chicago, & Akron

Of course, there were many other cities and numerous random publishers during this 100-year period publishing Napoleon books, but we will conclude this survey with Boston, Chicago, and Akron.

Among the Boston publishers, ending up at the third main location for the industry, the major publishing event was Houghton Mifflin Company's editions of Theodore Ayrault Dodge's four-volume *Napoleon*, a part of its Great Captain series, published in 1904 (and reissued in later editions) and printed by The Riverside Press in Cambridge, Massachusetts. Dodge was used by scholars and by cadets at West Point (my edition from 1932 was owned by Cadet Samuel, including a test review sheet from 1938). The set totals 2,720 pages (620, 546, 746, and 808 respectively). Other Houghton Mifflin titles included John Codman Ropes' *The First Napoleon: A Sketch, Political and Military* (1885), with four pages of ads in the back of the book including one for Dorsey Gardner's *Quatre Bras, Ligny, and Waterloo: A Narrative of the Campaign in Belgium*, selling for $5.

Meanwhile, several publishers in this city brought out editions of Hazlitt's *Napoleon*, including De Wolfe, Fiske & Co., in a three-volume set and Dana Estes & Company with a six-volume set (leather with green marbled boards and tissues, with decorative cover). The Napoleon Society headquartered here published a 16-volume set featuring six volumes of Hazlitt in 1895, along with four volumes of Bourrienne and six volumes of Junot in half-leather with marbled boards (one reference refers to an edition of only 500).

Roberts Brothers of Boston published a key work in 1892, *A Short History of Napoleon the First* by John Robert Seeley, printed by University Press (specifically by John Wilson and Son) in Cambridge. Finally, the most famous author publishing a Napoleon-related book in Boston wasn't a historian or Napoleon specialist, but none other than Ralph Waldo Emerson (1803-1882) when Phillips, Sampson, and Company issued *Representative Men* (1850), featuring a chapter on Napoleon; the book has never been out of print.

The W.B. Conkey Company of Chicago brought out an abridged version of John S.C. Abbott's Napoleon as *Napoleon Bonaparte and His Campaigns*, with 80 illustrations, for its Young People's Cloth Library (no date). Meanwhile, Chicago publisher A. C. McClurg and Company accepted the manuscript of a first lieutenant in the Second Cavalry, Herbert H. Sargent, writing *Napoleon Bonaparte's First Campaign: With Comments*, from his post in 1894 at Fort Bowie, Arizona. Thompson & Thomas Publisher of Chicago published an edition of Headley's *Napoleon and His Marshals* in 1861.

In Akron, Ohio, the Saalfield Publishing Co. published several popular works on Napoleon. Their books were printed by The Werner Company Book Manufacturers, and their titles included a popular biography series (with prices ranging from $1.25 to $4 in 1904) and a $1 each juvenile series (in 1904). *The Military Career of Napoleon the Great* by Chicago-based writer Montgomery B. Gibbs, was published in 1895, and re-issued at least once in 1902. With a leather spine (with the title Napoleon's Military Career), the 514-page book sold for $1.50 in 1902, featuring gilded top and rough page edges on the side and the bottom, and 32 black and white plates.

Also on the Saalfield list was John L. Stoddard's *Napoleon: From Corsica to St. Helena* (1894, re-issued 1900), a 260-page over-sized book that would today be labeled a coffee-table volume, featuring 330 black and white illustrations with an introduction and descriptions by Stoddard, who was also known for other "popular pictorial" books with this house. Saalfield also published a University Press Association edition of *Recollections of the Private Life of Napoleon* by Constant, translated by Walter Clark, in three volumes in 1904 (featuring the Napoleonic symbol of a bee on the blue binding) and the same set under their own imprint 1915.

Although our examination ends with the 100th anniversary of his death, it should be noted that the entire decade of the 1920s was active with Napoleonic biography, and artfully-produced books continued to appear as a matter of course into the 1930s.

5
AMERICAN BEST-SELLER

The paper "Emil Ludwig's Napoleon: The American Legacy of a German Biography" was delivered at the Michigan Academy of Science, Arts & Letters, March 11, 2011, at Saginaw Valley State University.

"Of the thousands of lives of Napoleon, Ludwig's comes closest to the goal of artful biography: which is to evoke a human being from the mists, to show his life unfolding so graphically that readers can see and sense him as a living person." – Stephen B. Oates [1]

It's a truly amazing biography; my favorite after more than four decades of reading about and studying Napoleon. The review in *The New Yorker* appearing with the release of the 1927 English translation (by Eden and Cedar Paul), said the book "is the first biography of the New Year" and "has every prospect of being first when this year ends." [2] Written in the present tense, this portrayal of Napoleon is alive and personal. Ludwig engages his reader with questions:

"What is Paris saying?"
"But where is the enemy?"
"What is to be done?"
"Suddenly he changes his mind. Why?"
"A terrible pause. What will happen?"
"What is he reading today?"

And his dramatic presentation sometimes answers those questions too: "Shall he use the Old Guard? Not yet! Not yet!" Responding to another situation, Ludwig writes what Napoleon was thinking: "Too soon. Better wait." He will set the scene, saying, "We are at..." providing wonderful descriptions of a room or geographic feature. "At Paris, in his study, Napoleon has a silent witness of his activities;

a bronze bust of Frederick the Great." The style is true biography, but also as engaging as story-telling.

There are no other biographies like it, unless you turn to his more than a dozen biographies, including treatments of Goethe, Jesus, Beethoven, Lincoln, and Franklin Roosevelt. Ludwig's masterpiece on Napoleon is important to us because it made No. 2 on the best-seller list in America in 1927; ranking higher on the best-seller list than any other Napoleonic biography. It was still on the best-seller list at the end of the following year at No. 4. Through various hardback and paper editions, the book was in print for five decades. Although now out-of-print, it is widely available in used bookshops and online (Advanced Book Exchange, www.abe.com, had 914 copies available as of October 31, 2011, ranging in price from $1 to $110). [3]

And it is a beautifully written book, probably the greatest example of true literature in Napoleonic biography, stressing the artful composition of a life, as biographer Stephen Oates says above. Secondly, especially for book-lovers, the early hardback edition is a wonderfully designed volume. This was also an important book for me personally, being the first grown-up biography I'd read on Napoleon. During high school, I read the Modern Library Edition, (#95 in the series), a small red hardback edition that came out in 1953. My first Napoleon biography was during elementary school with Landmark's *Napoleon and the Battle of Waterloo* by W. Frances Winwar). Since then, I've read Ludwig's book several times, used it as a text in a military science class I taught for Army ROTC, and have collected the various editions of the book – so I admit to a total lack of objectivity on this topic.

The work does, however, have its critics, but even the critics don't question Ludwig's flare for writing. Leo Gershoy calls the work "more readable than reliable." A prominent current-day critic is Alan Schom, author of *Napoleon Bonaparte*, named by *Library Journal* among the top five biographies of the year for 1997. In reply to my query for his opinion on Ludwig's *Napoleon*, Dr. Schom pointed out that Ludwig was not a historian and had no training in that field. "He wrote charming fictional history, including his work on Bonaparte.

Historically there is no basis for it, all 'the facts' he gives are his imagined version, except for the dates involved: birth/death, famous battles. No bona fide university research library keeps Ludwig in its history section." [4]

There are other historians who don't quite share my enthusiasm. Dr. David A. Bell, professor of History at Princeton, acknowledges that Ludwig's book "was certainly widely read in the twenty years or so after its publication, but it pretty much fell out of sight as far as academics are concerned, and by this point it has been so long, that even most Napoleon specialists don't know the book." He cited the database of journal articles, JSTOR, with 260 citations to Ludwig in the 1930's, 205 in the 1940's, and only 74 in the 1950's, after which the number continued declining to only 36 in the past decade. He also shared an interesting reference, an 'ngram graph' in Google Books (http://ngrams.googlelabs.com). [5]

But there are fans, as we shall discover, not just because of how the book brought Napoleon to life for generations of readers, but also how it was appreciated by authorities in the study of biography for its style, or art form.

Ludwig's Life & Workshop

Ludwig (1881-1948) grew up in Breslau, Germany. The family name was Cohn, but his Jewish parents gave him a new last name "to offset the difficulties attending possession of an obviously Jewish name." He was intrigued by the story his father told him about the day his father saw Bonaparte. A vase depicting the general adorned the Ludwig home and Emil collected portraits of Napoleon and visited his tomb in Paris. He was educated at Breslau University and then earned a law degree from Heidelberg University, but decided against a career in the law. His early love of drama and poetry would guide his development after brief stints in the law and business. When he was 24 years-old he wrote a play about Napoleon. He and his German-Scottish wife Elga Wolff built a home in the mountains of Switzerland – Moscia was the home's name – on Lake Maggiore in Ascona. Emil and Elga had two children. They established citizenship there in 1932 and made it their permanent home to escape the dangers of anti-Semitic actions when the Nazis came to power. Before the First World War he worked in London writing for a German newspaper and during the war he worked in the German Ministry of Information. From that time on he made his living as a writer. [6]

He wrote two biographies before the First World War – about the German poet Richard Dehmel and the composer Wagner (both coming out in 1913) – but his first significant biography was on Goethe (1920) and Ludwig became a pioneer in the New School of Biography or the New Biography, exploring the inner life of the subject. In his memoir, *Gifts of Life: A Retrospect* (1931), Ludwig (published on the eve of his 50th birthday) wrote in a chapter titled "My Workshop." He described how he began his task by studying portraits, sculptures, and masks of his subjects, reading letters and books (from 100 to 300 source books), and then – using his skills as a dramatist – developing 'scenes' for his books. He wrote at least two printed pages daily and typically worked on his books from March to October. He brought his subjects to life by focusing on their age and not on the dates (which reminds me of Ida Tarbell's inclusion of age along with dates in the chronology of her Napoleon). [7]

In *Genius and Character* (1927), Ludwig wrote that he was inspired by Plutarch, whom he called a portraitist, by Plutarch's philosophy of telling the interior life of a historic figure. Plutarch wrote:

> "As portrait-painters are more exact in the lines and features of the face, in which the character is seen, than in the other parts of the body, so I must be allowed to give my more particular attention to the marks and indications of the souls of men, and while I endeavor by these to portray their lives, may be free to leave more weighty matters and great battles to be treated by others." [8]

According to Ludwig, "Our educational intent is to show all readers, and especially youth, that great men are not gods, that they have been gripped by the same all-too-human passions, repressions, and encumbrances as afflict every other mortal, and that they have fought through, regardless, to their goal." [9]

The Book

Ludwig was 45-years-old when he wrote *Napoleon*, telling his story in five sections, with each part beginning with a quote from Johann Wolfgang von Goethe, and a chronology at the beginning of the volume to help the reader follow the sequence of his story. There is also a Goethe quote opposite the title page, "Napoleon went forth to seek Virtue, but, since she was not to be found, he got Power."

Book One, The Island (1769-1796) – from birth to his command of the Army of Italy and marriage to Josephine Beauharnais – begins with, "The story of Napoleon produces on me an impression like that produced by the Revelation of Saint John the Divine. We all feel there must be something more in it, but we do not know what." - Goethe

Book Two, The Torrent (1796-1799) – from the Italian Campaign through being named First Consul – begins with, "So divine an illumination is always linked with youth and productivity; and, in very truth, Napoleon was one of the most productive men that ever lived." - Goethe

Book Three, The River (1800-1811) – from the Battle of Marengo to the birth of Napoleon II – begins with "One who thoughtfully ponders the centuries, Surveys the whole in the clear light of the spirit; All that is petty has vanished from sight; Oceans and continents alone are of account." - Goethe

Book Four, The Sea (1812-1815) – covering the Russian Campaign through Waterloo and its aftermath – begins, "It is essential that this man shall be ruined! But since, here below everything takes place by natural causes, the daemons trip him; thus, in the end, even Napoleon is overthrown." - Goethe

Book Five, The Rock (1815-1821) – focusing on his captivity and death on St. Helena – begins with: "On Judgment Day, before God's throne, There stood at last, Napoleon. The Devil had his list begun, Of crimes the Bonapartes had done, When God the Father, or God the Son, Cut Satan short before God's throne: 'Don't bore us all to death with reading, A German professorial pleading! If you're bold enough to face him, In your kingdom you may place him." - Goethe

The final three pages of the book consist of a section titled "Envoy," explaining the nature of the work. "To examine this man's inner life; to explain his resolves and his refraining, his deeds and his sufferings, his fancies and his calculations, as issuing from the moods of his heart – the disclosure of this *great chain of affects* [Ludwig's emphasis], was at once the means and the end of the portrayal." He explains that there are differences in the skills of a historian and biographer – the "art of portrayal." Ludwig makes it clear that he does not approve of the "historical novel," saying how both Goethe and Napoleon himself thought these "confuse everything." He explains that events that occurred on the same day, whether affairs of state or personal, are treated on the same page because they are connected. He argues that everything he writes is historically accurate "except the soliloquies." [10]

The author's acknowledgements at the very end of the book thanks Edouard Driault, editor of the Revue des Etudes Napoleoniennes, Versailles, and F. M. Kircheisen "for kindly help in supplying material for the illustrations" and thanks to Professor Pariset of Strasburg and Kurt Wildhagen of Heidelberg "for advice during the preparation of this book."

On the back of the brick-red jacket from an early edition of the book is a statement that the work "has been adopted as required reading by Professor Charles Seymour of Yale University for his course in Napoleonic History," followed by review excerpts. Harry Salpeter of the *New York World* wrote, "Almost might I say that I have lived with Napoleon…in the hours during which I read this book and in other hours the image of Napoleon haunted me. With Ludwig the reader sees Napoleon from within. It is an internal view we get, a view in which we are emotionally involved." According to the *Brooklyn Times*, "It makes a strong appeal both to the scientifically trained scholar who demands strictest historical accuracy as well as to the general reader who appreciates a work of art." The inside flaps contain 18 more tributes which are provided in the "Reviews" section of this chapter.

Selected Readings

It would be impossible to convey the spirit of this biography without providing some highlights of Ludwig's artful writing:

On St. Helena: "The sea spreads out into the vast distance. It is like a mirror of steel. The man on the rock, hands clasped behind, stares across the watery plain. He is lonely, so lonely." Another St. Helena scene: "The Emperor rises as late as possible, so that the day may seem shorter...Napoleon asks about the weather...Sometimes there is no sugar to sweeten the coffee. Has the mailship come to port with fresh newspapers? Nothing as yet. Gourgaud arrives and writes from dictation. Where were we? The pyramids. The Emperor paces to and fro in the narrow room; a map of Egypt lies spread on the table." [11]

On History: "History inspires him. While with rapid strokes he is making history, history gives his spirit wings. In boyhood, he had studied Plutarch; as lieutenant, he had read the history of all times; now, from moment to moment, he turns the knowledge to account...Time-honored figures are ever present to his imagination; he wants to resemble them, to outdo them." [12]

On Maps: "Through all countries, for the whole duration of his life, the map follows him, pierced with colored pins, illuminated at night by 20 or 30 candles, and with a pair of compasses lying on it. This is his altar, before which he offers up his prayers. It is the real home for the man who has no home." [13]

The Editions

The earliest edition I own is the 14th printing (April 1928), by New York publisher Boni & Liveright. This 707-page edition, with an illustration of Napoleon's profile facing a map of Europe, carries the sub-title "The Man of Destiny" (but the book does not officially have a sub-title) and identifies this volume as the Fourteenth Large Edition. Inside are 21 black and white illustrations spread throughout the book, wide margins around the pages, and unique page headings describing in a few words something from that page – something no longer seen in publishing.

For those who may not find an edition complete with illustrations, they include the artists: Pontornini, Jean Guerin, Jacques Louis David, Wocher, Andre Dutertre, Girodet, J.D.A. Ingres, Alexandre Tardieu after a drawing by Jean Baptiste Isabey, Vigneux, bust by Houdon, woodcut by J.P. Droz, Bourgeois after a painting by David, Horace Vernet, engraving by Robert Lefevre, and the deathmask by Dr. Antommarchi.

Garden City Publishing Company (Garden City, New York) came out with a less expensive and smaller volume, but the same number of pages. The inside flap of the dust jacket (designed by Edward A. Wilson) explains that the book was printed from the same plates of the original edition and that Ludwig accepted a reduced royalty. Modern Library's edition came out in 1953 for $1.25, with the inside dust jacket declaring, "Of the vast library of books devoted to the deeds and personality of Napoleon Bonaparte, non has had such an immense popular success as Emil Ludwig's vibrant biography."

"The reason is not far to seek," continues the jacket. "Upon the framework of historical fact, Ludwig has re-created the whole miraculous cycle of Napoleon's life and has imbued it with the passion and imagination that motivated"...his career. "It is a book of courage and violence, as vivid and as stirring as Napoleon's victories and ultimate humiliation." This edition – No. 95 in the Modern Library series – is 703 pages and lacks the individual page headings.

Meanwhile, the 1932 Garden City Publishers edition of another book (*The Autobiography of Benvenuto Cellini*, a part of the Star Series for $1) was still promoting Ludwig's *Napoleon*, featuring that title across the top of the inside of the dust jacket saying it is "one of the greatest books of modern times."

Pocket Books brought out their first paperback edition in 1953 followed by its Giant Cardinal paper edition a year later selling for 50 cents and this was reissued at least twice in that format with the third printing in 1961. The 656-page book features a cover illustration of Napoleon and his staff observing a battle by Tom Dunn. On the back cover is an excerpt from the *Philadelphia Public Ledger*, "Read Emil Ludwig's, for your reward will indeed be great! It is one of the most fascinating and richly satisfying of modern biographies." The 1965 Pocket edition sold for 75 cents.

Another paper edition by Pocket Books came out, using the same plates, but in a slightly larger format and by 1972 was in its 6th printing. The first page carries four new review excerpts of the book not previously used in earlier editions. "It's a vivid piece of portraiture, a glowing tribute to the genius of the man of destiny," from the *American Political Science Review.*

"The book will have, and deserves, a tremendous vogue," according to *The Nation.* "It has the proper amount of…spicy anecdote and humor and genuine understanding…to make it a popular biography and to win hearty approbation from the literary critics." *The New York Times* called it, "A portrait, for the most part sympathetic, many-sided and exceedingly vivid." Finally, the *Saturday Review* said, "With brilliant success it attempts the difficult task of giving the inner history of Napoleon."

In 1970, *Reader's Digest* included a condensed version of Ludwig's Napoleon in its one-volume *Family Treasury of Great Biographies*, with Ludwig's story comprising 263 pages, or almost half of the volume (25 of those pages being illustrations, but not the original illustrations from 1926). "Napoleon, in truth, was full of contradictions. Invincible in battle almost to the end, he could be the helpless captive of a woman's charms," according to the one-page introduction to the excerpt. "Dictatorial in his use of power, the framework of law and government he set up in the Code Napoleon was so wisely conceived that much of it still governs France today."

Finally, you can view a variety of these book covers at: www.LibraryThing.com.

The Legacy

Albert Guerard, wrote in 1956 that Ludwig "remains the most readable" while citing general works, also noting that some of Ludwig's collaborators were "excellent guides (Kircheisen, Driault, and Pariset, but could not speak to Wildhagen's reputation). Steven Englund, New York University professor of History and author of

Napoleon: A Political Life, wrote in 2004 that Ludwig's work did have a novelesque quality but is "quite astonishing" with "remarkable literary and intellectual brilliance." J. David Markham says this work "was the first widely available translated book on Napoleon, and perhaps the first that did not reflect the British slant on Napoleonic history. For many in my generation, it played a significant role in the early development of our understanding of Napoleon." [14]

Sifting through interviews of various historians yields some interesting revelations about the impact of this biography. Historian Stephen Ambrose recalled "being caught up in the sweep and the drama" of Ludwig's story-telling. Napoleonic historian and University of South Carolina professor Lt. Col. Owen "Mike" Connelly (Ret.), had read Ludwig's Napoleon by the time he graduated from high school at the age of 16. And Dr. Donald D. Horward, founder of the Institute on Napoleon and the French Revolution at Florida State University, also found early inspiration in Ludwig's book during high school (along with Phillip Gaudella's work on Wellington). [15]

The Genre

Ludwig's unique style of focusing on the personality of the subject is mentioned in several works on the study of biography. Writing in 1948, Marston Balch, professor of English at Tufts College, said "One of the most interesting methods of presenting a subject's life has been developed by Ludwig and widely imitated in America," further observing that this method "is capable of giving tremendous sweep, contrast, climax, and event suspense." [16]

Donald J. Winslow addresses two attributes often associated with Ludwig's style. Discussing literary biography, he wrote in 1995 that today the term "generally applies to any biography or autobiography with literary qualities, regardless of the professional field of the subject." According to Winslow, the term 'New Biography' refers to experimental life-writing between 1918-1939, with the biographer's "stress on artistic design, novelistic form, psychological interpretation, and dramatic sequences…" citing – along with Ludwig – Lytton Strachey, Andre Maurois, and Stefan Zweig. [17]

Ruth Hoberman wrote in 2001 that the term 'new biography' "emerged to describe the biographical experiments" that followed Lytton Strachey's *Eminent Victorians*, "best epitomized" by Strachey's own *Queen Victoria*, with the trend including Andre Maurois in France, Ludwig in Germany, and Harold Nicholson in England – "all of whom speculated freely about their subject's inner lives, assuming them to be shaped by unconscious motives better discerned by their biographers than by themselves." [18]

Other comments include authorities in the study of biography: Hermione Lee saying Ludwig was "driven by an intuitive search for the essence of character;" Edgar Johnson defends Ludwig's use of "conversations" in the narrative; while Carl Rollyson has reservations with this style of 'new biography.' He observes that these biographers presents their subjects "in dramatic relief" with figures "emerging boldly out of their periods, dominating their times by force of personality." According to Rollyson, this approach detaches "character from history, in so far as they were willing to go beyond the documented record." [19]

Reviews

Although a bit unconventional, I've decided not to bury these review snippets in our notes section. Given the desire to know how the public was viewing Napoleon (and Ludwig's fine writing), here are excerpts from the inside flap of the book jacket from the 1928 edition of *Napoleon*:

Will Durant: "I congratulate you on bringing out so necessary a book, by so competent and brilliant a man and in such a substantial form."

Atlantic Monthly: "An outstanding book in Napoleonic literature – a Sargent portrait wherein secrets that ordinarily lie hidden in the heart are written in the countenance for all the world to read. May prove to be an abiding contribution to the world's creative literature."

Emporia Gazette: "Head and shoulders above the new books is 'Napoleon,' perhaps without equal among the many Napoleon biographies. It is fine because it is human, and it's easy, clear style brings out Napoleon as no book of history has done."

Independent: "A remarkable biography and an intensely vivid and interesting book."

Providence Journal: "The final effects of the book are to leave the reader, perhaps for the first time, with a clean-cut and convincing picture of the man. No book-lover will be happy in knowing that this book is abroad if he hasn't it in his own library."

World's Work "Ludwig has produced a genuine masterpiece. His book is like a reel of instantaneous flash pictures. Not since Lord Rosebery's *Napoleon: The Last Phase* have I seen anything better," wrote Thomas L. Masson.

Washington Star: "More stirring than any novel could be, this study nevertheless has all the qualities of the novel plus the reality of a great character of history besides. The author is a genius of sympathetic appreciation, of poetic imagination, of historic accuracy, of dramatic sense of proportion."

Philadelphia Public Ledger: "Read Emil Ludwig's 'Napoleon,' for your reward will indeed be great! It is one of the most fascinating and richly satisfying of modern biographies," wrote Starr Lawrence.

The Cincinnati Inquirer: "Great, and intensely fascinating."

New York Evening Post: "Emil Ludwig's biography of Napoleon is the best that has been written to date," wrote Dr. Joseph Collins.

American Mercury: "A biography of the first order; complete, accurate, well-written and felicitously translated – a psychological biography rather than a history, with the techniques and charm of a romance."

New York Herald Tribune: "It is an admirable book in every respect; sane and generous, well-composed, well written and most felicitously translated. In its sustained level of excellence, in its balance of widely different merits, in the universality of its appeal, it stands not very far below the greatest."

Living Age: "The book is enthralling from end to end."

Kansas City Star: "After reading it, one feels that one has at last come in touch with the man that was Napoleon. Out of the crash of battle and the bewildering maze of political events, the human figure of Napoleon has at length emerged."

The New York Telegram: "Not in years have we heard a book discussed in so many circles and diversified groups as Ludwig's 'Napoleon.' And without exception, it is thoroughly liked. Ludwig has made the biography race along at tremendous speed. We recommend it unqualifiedly," wrote S. Jay Kaufman.

The Philadelphia Public Ledger: "One of the most fascinating and richly satisfying of modern biographies."

The New Republic: "Mr. Ludwig comes as near to the heart of the mystery as anyone imaginable could. An astounding and overwhelming feat, fair-minded, penetrating, a most solid rearrangement of the richest treasury of relevant facts, quotations, documents," wrote Robert Littell.

The Brooklyn Eagle: "The books among books – on Napoleon," wrote George Currie.

Atheus Banner Herald: "Here is a book that holds me breathless. Whenever I pick it up I want to keep right on reading it, even after the last call for dinner."

Postscript

During World War II, the Ludwigs lived in Southern California and went on tour in the U.S. while working on his biographies of Abraham Lincoln and Franklin Roosevelt. They returned to their home in Switzerland after the war where he died of a heart attack three years later.

Felix E. Hirsch wrote about his friend of 30 years following Ludwig's death in 1948, publishing his personal recollections in *Books Abroad: An International Literary Quarterly*. "Young students to whom I have recommended his Goethe, his Napoleon, and his Bismarck – the three of his biographical studies which I consider his noblest achievements – have never complained about the assignment; they gained from his books the inspiration which was so sadly lacking in many more thorough scholarly monographs," wrote Hirsch. In this reflective piece, he referenced responses Ludwig gave to an interviewer: What do you consider the basic trait of your character? Serenity was the answer. Which quality do you treasure most highly? Productivity was the answer. [20]

According to the final chapter of *Gifts of Life*, "Extract from My Son's Diary," Emil Ludwig "was happiest out of doors with flowers, dogs, and us." [21].

Perhaps the most fitting end for this essay, though, comes from Ludwig's "Envoy" section of his *Napoleon*. Summing up Napoleon's life, he writes: "What a man can attain through self-confidence and courage, through passion and imagination, through industry and will, he attained." [22]

And Ludwig's biography tells that story better than any other, confirmed by the American consumer.

6
TEACHING NAPOLEON

Adapted from the presentation "Teaching Napoleon: Lecture Outline and Course Syllabus" presented at the Michigan Academy of Science, Arts & Letters on March 26, 2010, at Calvin College, Grand Rapids.

> "A thorough study of the times and the career of Napoleon Bonaparte is essential to an understanding of the present world...The story of Napoleon needs to be retold for each successive generation." – Ida M. Tarbell [1]

> "In approaching Napoleon, we should try to strike a balance between the man and his world, the individual and his culture, the ruler and his collaborators. Napoleon was not a man out of time but a man *of* his time whose extraordinary career reflected and shaped his age." – Rafe Blaufarb [2]

Teaching about Napoleon has the same challenge as writing about him; it is overwhelming because of the scope and amount of material. It doesn't seem to matter how much you know about him, the task of lecturing on or teaching about Napoleon is a challenge whether your audience is the general public or high school or college students.

Things have changed, of course, because of the internet, impacting audiences of all ages. When I was in elementary school and you wanted to know about Napoleon, the school librarian would direct you to the wonderful Landmark series and you would discover *Napoleon and the Battle of Waterloo* by Frances Winwar, with illustrations by David Stone (1953). Or, we would rely on the old reliable *World Book Encyclopedia*. Today, elementary students benefit from resources such as the lesson plan available to their teacher via the web-based Lessonsnips. This site features a lesson plan geared for 4th and 5th graders on Napoleon, with a focus on how he came to power, why the Russian Campaign ended in disaster, the outcome of Waterloo, and where he spent his time in exile (www.lessonsnips.com/lesson/napoleon).

Young readers (or teachers) may also check out the Kids' Corner of the website of the Foundation Napoleon, which invites younger children and teens to "play and learn with timelines, maps, quizzes, games, fact-files, news, book, and exhibits. The site even has sections broken down by age groups for the youngest students: Age 3-plus, Napoleon at his country house; Age 6-plus, Napoleon and his family; and Age 10-plus, In the Footsteps of Napoleon, etc (www.napoleon.org). There is also the website The Time Warp Trio.com with adventures including Napoleon. And Charles MacKay wrote the article, "The Trial of Napoleon: A Case Study for Using Mock Trials" in the Fall 2000 issue of *Teaching History*.

Earlier generations than mine had resources available to them also. The Instructor Literature Series featured the 31-page *Story of Napoleon* by Bertha E. Bush (1911), one of 353 volumes in this "limp cloth" series (a durable paperback). One the most interesting examples of instructional tools was *The Mentor*, published weekly by The Mentor Association, an institution of learning established for the development of a popular interest in art, literature, science, history, nature, and travel. Among their taglines: Learn one thing every day, Efficiency & Knowledge, and Make the spare moment count. *The Mentor's* Department of Biography brought out No. 38 on November 3, 1913, "Napoleon Bonaparte," by journalist and historian Ida M. Tarbell. The 11-page booklet was accompanied by six suitable-for-framing black and white illustrations, with descriptions of the scene depicted on the backside. "It is nearly a hundred years since he dropped out of active life; but his story is more rather than less thrilling as time goes on," writes Tarbell.

During the 1920s, those pursuing lifelong learning had the Little Blue Book ten-cent pocket series edited by E. Haldeman-Julius, "A University in Print," with each little booklet numbering about 60 pages. The series included four lessons on Napoleon: *Life of Napoleon* by Charles J. Finger, *The Empire of Napoleon* by Louis R. Gottschalk, *Maxims of Napoleon*, and *Battle of Waterloo* by Hugo. Speaking of lifelong learning, another opportunity for teaching Napoleon, in addition to a single talk to a community group or classroom or a semester-long college class, are the emerging short courses offered for free by colleges with lifelong learning programs. A mix of the two outlines provided below could assist in preparing for a half-day seminar or two or three-session class.

The Lecture

Where do you start? How can you cover any facet of his life in an hour? And what's the best approach to keep the momentum and focus throughout a semester? The purpose of this presentation is to provide an outline and some resources for such undertakings. Preparing for a guest-lecturer appearance for a high school class in 2003, I sent out a call for help on the "Napoleon-Series" website's discussion forum. Titled "Conversational Information on Napoleon" – thus setting the theme for an informal and hopefully entertaining talk – I received some interesting advice:

Focus on three different phases of his life, said one respondent: General Bonaparte, the Son of the Revolution, stressing the "astonishing" Italian Campaign and Egyptian campaign, with emphasis on the scientific mission; Napoleon Bonaparte, First Consul, stressing Napoleon as administrator, the Codes, and his establishment of the 'modern state;' concluding with Napoleon I, the Emperor. "Don't forget to say that even if it seems his life ended at St. Helena, thanks to 15 years of his meteoric life, his ideas eventually win." Another wrote: "Start with the statement that the wars from 1792-1815 cost France about one million dead (regardless of who was responsible for those deaths) to give them an idea that this is not about nice uniforms and glory of a person." This respondent also thought I should mention Napoleon's massacre of prisoners-of-war during the Egyptian campaign – but also creation of the Civil Code.

One respondent, who taught 8th grade history, recommended focusing on his personality (strengths and weaknesses) and his being a self-made man. Throw in some interesting anecdotes. Other responses included the importance of showing illustrations, emphasizing his age at various points during his career, explaining some of the myths (hand-in-vest, height), and even including

Josephine to help make his life come alive. Several respondents suggested concluding the lecture with some mysteries of his death: the alleged poisoning and the rumors about his body being switched at death, with the real Napoleon escaping from captivity.

Having given several talks to high school, college, and general public audiences, I've learned that you cannot even summarize his life or career in an hour and trying to do so is as uncomfortable for you as it is for the audience. And as much trouble as it is sometimes to use PowerPoint, it is worth it. I tried to speak on Waterloo once in lecture format, and I would have been better served showing them paintings and maps so they could feel that they were there.

Possible titles include Napoleon Reconsidered, Napoleon Revisited, The Relevance of Napoleon, Why Napoleon Matters, or The Legacy of Napoleon. Handouts should include at least a chronology. If you can find it, the one in Ida Tarbell's *A Short Life of Napoleon Bonaparte* (1896) includes a column with his age for each year. Students are especially surprised at what Napoleon had done at the age they currently are.

Sometimes it helps to read passages of great works for dramatic affect; works of true literature. In addition to some of the passages shared in Chapter 5 from Ludwig, I recommend the opening page from H.A.L. Fisher's 1912 masterpiece, *Napoleon* ("As we think of Napoleon Bonaparte what a world of visions and memories rises before the mind…"). Also, the opening section of Steven Englund's 2004 *Napoleon: A Political Life* – the section called "Frisson" about Napoleon's tomb. Also, Philip Dwyer (*Napoleon: The Path to Power*) – portions of the Prologue: The Bridge at Arcola and the section In Search of Bonaparte in the Epilogue.

If you are offering a half-day workshop and need a general handout, consider the 159-page *Napoleon: My Ambition Was Great* by Thierry Lentz in the Discoveries Series (2004), lavishly illustrated ($12.95). Mike Rapport's *The Napoleonic Wars: A Very Short Introduction* (Oxford University Press, 2013), also offers makes a useful resource for teaching at 149 pages.

Here is a sample outline for your lecture:

Introduction

- Why Napoleon? Who cares?
- Discuss the relevance of this topic for you, the speaker (how did you become interested in Napoleon?).
- How he and his times were influenced by the French Revolution. The lack of this perspective is a common complaint by academic historians toward many of us who tend to focus primarily on Napoleon as a personality, while lacking the full context of European and French history.

Mental Images

- His hat, his stance, his stare (many references to his eyes)
- Napoleon as a brand (Google Napoleon and advertising)
- Snapshots (actual images or descriptions)
- Crossing the Alps (on a mule, not a horse like David's famous painting)
- Return from Elba (not a shot fired!)
- Sailing to Exile
- Missing his wife, son, and family on St. Helena.

Relevance in American Popular Culture

- Google searches on Napoleon
- Napoleon in advertising
- Self-made man and the American tradition
- Place-names (locations, and people named after him)

Example of the Great Man Theory

This theory continues to be disliked by many academic historians, but here goes:

- Defined his age
- Greatest soldier ever?
- Civil Code

- A United Europe?
- Aspects of his life:
  - Leadership
  - Campaigns
  - Work ethic
  - A day in the life
  - Family
- His leadership team (senior staff and Marshals)
- Art of War
- The influence of commissioned art
- Books, autographs, re-enactments, societies, websites

Legacy

- In his footsteps
- Good vs. bad?
- Judgments?
- Alternate history (what if he had stayed in power and unified much of Europe or what if he had escaped to America?
- Cause of death (conspiracy theories)
- Multiplier effect: his battlefield presence worth 40,000 men
- The admiration his opposition had for him (especially the British)
- His place in American pop culture

The College Course

Most university history departments offer an undergrad course titled the French Revolution & Napoleon, taught annually or at least every other year. In the case of more specialized programs, such as online history degrees from Norwich University or the American Military University, there may be actual courses focusing exclusively on Napoleon. The classic Napoleon biography by Felix Markham remains in print today in paper to a large degree because of its use as a college text; the most recent edition includes an afterward by historian Steven Englund.

I asked two history professors for their opinion about teaching Napoleon and the reaction of students to the topic. Dr. Judith Stone taught "French Revolution and Napoleon" at Western Michigan University and later at Portland State University, and reports that the class always filled to its maximum capacity. She shared that earlier in her career at Western, she would have some students taking the course to fulfill requirements for Army ROTC, and "they were, of course, interested in what made Napoleon such a successful general."

More recently, she reports, "I think students are more critical of Napoleon. Many comment negatively on his abandonment of his troops in Egypt and Russia, and also the extremely inadequate supplies and equipment during both those campaigns." Regarding the relevance of teaching about Napoleon today, she says "this period serves as an example of the negative consequences to state and society when legitimacy is based on military conquest. I have to confess that my assessment of Napoleon grows increasingly negative every time I teach the period. I now label his domestic policies as 'paternalist' and, of course, his foreign policies as 'imperial conquests." [3]

Like at Western, "French Revolution and Napoleon" is offered at Kalamazoo College every other year, and also typically fills up. According to Dr. David Barclay, students seem to be more interested in the French Revolution than Napoleon. As of this date (2008), he reported that "astonishingly, there are relatively few good recent English-language biographies that are appropriate for classroom use. In recent years, I've stuck with the old warhorse by Felix Markham and the newer warhorse by Paul Johnson." So far as engaging student interest in Napoleon, he says it's in the context of the ancient consolidator vs. betrayer of the Revolution debate.

"Moreover, we have a generation of students now that has been taught to reject 'Great Man' approaches to history, especially if those individuals lived more than 50 years ago, so Napoleon doesn't seem to resonate too much with them," he says. As to the relevance of teaching Napoleon today, Barclay says, "I tend to argue that he is the first modern dictator, by which I mean he was the first to use the trappings of plebiscitary democracy, technologically-based state coercion, and pseudo-democratic legitimation to sustain an authoritarian regime in a democratic age...Both Bonapartism and

Caesarism are alive and well, as countries from Russia to South Africa remind us, and in that context Napoleon's legacy is very much with us." [4]

U.S. Military Academy

Captain Steven L. Delvaux, an instructor in the Department of History at West Point, New York, at the time of my contact in 2000, explains how his opening pitch to cadets is how Napoleon "changed forever the way that war is fought (particularly the scale and speed of warfare)," and his closing pitch focused on "his lasting doctrinal and theoretical contributions (i.e., Principles of War, and Theory of War) via Clausewitz and Jomini whose studies were both based on Napoleon's campaigns.

Delvaux would then stress to his cadets two major points or lessons "that we can take from Napoleon and still apply today, both primarily center around the concept of leadership: "The first is charisma," explains the infantry captain. "There are numerous stories of the affection of the soldiers of the Grande Army for Napoleon. The Imperial Guard's courageous final stand at Waterloo is perhaps the finest example."

The second major point the captain would stress in his classes was Napoleon's professionalism. Napoleon didn't achieve by accident, argues Delvaux, but was the consummate professional. "I point out the considerable time that he spent studying his craft as a cadet and junior officer. He was a voracious reader and, as I point out to the cadets, what is important is not the number of books he read, but what books he read and how he read them, i.e., with a critical mind, pen in hand, jotting notes in the margin" while critiquing the campaigns of Alexander, Caesar, and Frederick the Great.

Another lesson Delvaux taught his students was that Napoleon inspired such loyalty and devotion from his subordinates because "they recognized that he knew what he was doing...in an era when many military leaders were chosen on the basis of birth, Napoleon personified one of the basic tenets of the French Revolution concerning being judged based on merit. In that aspect, it was a perfect match of the man and the moment." [5]

U.S. Army Command & General Staff College

According to Lt. Col. E. L. Bowie, of the Combat Studies Institute at Fort Leavenworth, Kansas, in 2000, Napoleon is rarely, if ever, mentioned by name within the leadership curriculum, but "he has nevertheless influenced its development in ways of which the instructors themselves are probably unaware."

Bowie, responding to my query since he had served as both a Leadership and Military History instructor, believes that perhaps his most profound influence resides in the second and third-order theories and concepts his career inspired, citing both Carl Von Clausewitz and Antoine Jomini who "continue to frame and animate virtually all serious military thought." "Indeed, the rise of the General Staff itself, and by extension, the schools in which its members are trained are themselves a reaction of the other early 19th century powers to the challenge posed by Napoleon's genius for war," wrote Bowie. He concludes his response, saying "A thorough grounding in the career and influence of Napoleon remains fundamental to a coherent understanding of the current evolution of military art." [6]

Army War College

The Army War College, Carlisle Barracks, Penn., reported using Napoleon in several ways in its curriculum. In addition to their theory classes on Clausewitz and Jomini drawing heavily on Napoleon, several of their electives at that time included the study of Napoleon in a variety of ways. One example was highlighted by Col. Mike Matheny, director of the Advanced Strategic Art Program in 2000. His program offered a three-hour class on the Napoleonic Wars and conducted a staff ride to Europe on the Waterloo campaign. "We spend a good deal of time studying Clausewitz and Jomini – two classical theorists which still have great value, indeed, still very much influence our doctrine and strategic thinking today…"

"More importantly," continued Matheny, "a study of Napoleon and his wars helps to demonstrate the recurring patterns in warfare and the consistent nature of strategic behavior." He added that, "Napoleon and his times provide a laboratory from which modern military students can ponder the impact of personality, coalition warfare, policy, and strategy." Matheny concluded, writing that Napoleon "will be well worth the study of the serious student of war and relevant as long as nations use force and employ violence in pursuit of policy." [7]

Recommended Course

Here is a sample outline for an upper-level undergraduate course exclusively on Napoleon for a class that meets once-a-week. Electronic discussion forums, quizzes, and exams are not shown.

Course title options (other than just Napoleon) could include Introduction to Napoleon, The Life of Napoleon or The Study of Napoleon.

This could easily be offered as a graduate-level class with some additional readings, such as readings from Charles Esdaile, *Napoleon's Wars: An International History, 1803-1815* and David A. Bell, *The First Total War: Napoleon's Europe and the Birth of Warfare as We Know It*. For more of a biographical focus for his rise to power, you could include Philip Dwyer's *Napoleon: The Path to Power* (his prologue and the epilogue are exceptional. The sequel, *Citizen Emperor: Napoleon in Power*, is due out in November 2013).

Required textbooks
(currently available in paperback):

Steven Englund, *Napoleon: A Political Life*, 2004 (575 pages).

Rafe Blaufarb, *Napoleon: Symbol for an Age: A Brief History with Documents*, 2008 (233 pages).

Rafe Blaufarb and Claudia Liebeskind, *Napoleonic Foot Soldiers and Civilians: A Brief History with Documents*, 2011 (164 pages).

Additional texts could include two classics still available in paper

Felix Markham, *Napoleon* (the recent edition with an afterward by Steven Englund), and J. Christopher Herold, *The Age of Napoleon*. For a campaign focus you could use *The Wars of Napoleon* by Albert Sidney Britt III, in The West Point Military History Series (under series editor Thomas E. Griess), 2003, which is available in paper and is a concise 165 pages. Another addition could be *Napoleon Bonaparte* by Gregory Fremont-Barnes in the Leadership, Strategy, Conflict Series by Osprey, 2010, available in paper at 64 pages.

Course Pack
(222 pages of out-of-print sources):

Walter Geer, "The Personality of Napoleon," pp. 357-368, *Napoleon the First* (1921).

Emil Ludwig, "The Rock," pp. 545-606 and "Envoy," pp. 679-682, *Napoleon* (1926).

John J. Putman, "Napoleon," pp. 142-189, *National Geographic* (1982).

J. Holland Rose, "The Man," pp. 1-45, *Personality of Napoleon* (1912).

Lord Roseberry, "The Literature," pp. 1-8, "The Emperor at Home," pp. 164-179, *Napoleon: The Last Phase* (1902).

Hendrik Willem van Loon, "We Entertain Beethoven, Napoleon, and My Own Great-Grandfather and Listen to a Long Monologue," pp. 475-524, *Van Loon's Lives* (1942).

Course Objectives

Students will develop an appreciation of how Napoleon's military education, officer training, and early career – along with the influence of the French Revolution – shaped his rise to power. Students will enhance their understanding of how his leadership style and force of personality enabled him to become the leader of his country and project national power against the enemies of France, while also understanding how he failed at times to maintain peace and missed opportunities to stabilize Europe in France's favor. Students will understand the reasons for his fall from power and be able to discuss aspects of his legend and legacy. Readings and discussion will stimulate critical and creative thinking about key issues impacting his success and failure. Students will use historic documents to learn about Napoleon and his times and will give presentations on those aspects of his reign that resonate with their interests.

Course Outline

Course Introduction

-Lecture: Napoleon's Relevance
-Setting the stage: The French Revolution in context
-Course Overview

Napoleon: Reflections

-Englund: Frisson and the Introduction
-Ludwig: The Rock
-Blaufarb: Introduction, The Man and His Times
-Rose
-Geer
-Roseberry, The Literature

State of War

-Blaufarb: Documents: An Age of War
-Blaufarb & Liebeskind: Introduction: An Age of Total War?
-Blaufarb & Liebeskind: Documents: memoirs, recollections, diary, and journal.

Youth

-Englund: Book I

Rise to Power

-Englund: Book II
-Blaufarb: Documents: The Rise of Napoleon

Empire

-Englund: Book III
-Roseberry: Napoleon at Home
-Blaufarb: Documents: Napoleon in Power
-Blaufarb: Documents: Foundations of Napoleon's Regime

Decline and Downfall

-Englund: Book IV
-Blaufarb: Documents: Decline and Fall
-Blaufarb & Lieb: Documents (memoir)

Legacy & Legend

Ludwig: The Envoy
Putman
Van Loon

Student presentations

Student presentations could use documents from Blaufarb and Blaufarb/Liebeskind that were not included in the readings and also the suggested texts for use in a graduate version of this course. You could include a short lecture on a variety of topics on these student presentation days covering online resources; Napoleonic fiction, art and film, historic sites, museums, battlefields; and the nature of Napoleonic biography and the future of Napoleonic studies.

An interesting assignment for two students would be a comparison of the preface and epilogue in Alan Schom's 888-page *Napoleon Bonaparte* (1997) with the introduction and epilogue in J. David Markham's *Napoleon's Road to Glory: Triumphs, Defeats and Immortality* (2003) – contrasting the difference in each approach.

7
CHRONOLOGY

Adapted from the paper "Napoleon in America: A Chronology of Biographies, Place-Names, Relatives, and Exiles from 1815-1877" in the graduate seminar Early American History for the late (and inspiring professor) Dr. Peter Schmitt, Western Michigan University, 2003. This paper served as the originating idea for the pursuit of these essays.

1815: Following Waterloo, Napoleon is unable to escape to America as planned, but his older brother Joseph succeeds, living in Philadelphia before buying the Point Breeze estate on the Delaware River near Bordentown, New Jersey. He decorated the three-story mansion with hundreds of works of art including busts and statues by Canova and David's painting Napoleon Crossing the Alps. Mr. Bonaparte, as he was commonly called, also had a townhouse in Philadelphia, became a prominent citizen, and was elected to membership in the prestigious American Philosophical Society. See the chapters on Point Breeze in *The Gentle Bonaparte: A Biography of Joseph, Napoleon's Elder Brother* by Owen Connelly (1968) and in *The Bonapartes in America* by Clarence Edward Macartney and Gordon Dorrance (1939).

1816: Marshal Grouchy is the first prominent military official to arrive in Philadelphia, following Napoleon's exile. French exiles in that city organize for future pioneering expeditions that would be known as the French Agricultural & Manufacturing Society, the Society for Cultivation of the Vine & the Olive, and the French Emigrant Association.

1820: A play on Waterloo opens in New York City. "Thereafter the number of plays steadily increased, hitting a peak in the 1830s, but continuing until the Civil War," writes R. S. Alexander, in *Napoleon* (in the Arnold 'Reputation Series), New York: Oxford University Press, 2001, p. 163.

1827: Carey, Lea & Carey, the Philadelphia publishing house, brings out the first U.S. edition of Sir Walter Scott's *The Life of Napoleon Buonaparte* in three volumes (volume one 516 pages, volume two 399 pages, and volume three 368 pages). The author is actually listed as "by the author of Waverly," referring to his Waverly novels. The title pages note that the books were "stereotyped" by J. Howe.

1846: Writer Joel Tyler Headley's two-volume *Napoleon and His Marshals* was a best-seller with 50 reprints of the book. Portions of the work originally appeared in *American Review*.

1850: Ralph Waldo Emerson's *Representative Men* includes a chapter on "Napoleon: Man of the World."

1851: *Harper's Review* begins serialization in 37 installments of *The History of Napoleon Bonaparte* by John S. C. Abbott. The work is published in book format in 1855.

1852: Jerome Bonaparte (1830-1893), grandson of Napoleon's brother Jerome and his first wife Elizabeth Patterson (of Baltimore), graduates from the United States Military Academy at West Point. It is from Jerome's father Jerome "Bo" Bonaparte (1805-1870) and his wife Susan May Williams, "from whom the American Bonapartes descended," according to Desmond Seward (*Napoleon's Family*, 1986, p. 204).

1856: *Historic Doubts Relative to Napoleon Buonaparte, and Historic Certainties Respecting the Early History of America*, by Bishop Richard Whately is published by New York publisher Robert Carter & Brothers. The 184-page book argues that as extraordinary as Napoleon's career actually was – and people believe it – then how can so many people doubt the Gospels?

1861: Prince Napoleon, nephew to Napoleon (son of Napoleon's brother Jerome Napoleon and Catherine of Wurttemberg), visits America and witnesses the outbreak of the Civil War. The Prince visits New York, meets President Abraham Lincoln in Washington, D.C., and goes on to Philadelphia, Cleveland, Detroit, Mackinac Island, Mich., Milwaukee, Chicago, St. Louis, Niagara Falls, Quebec,

Montreal, and Boston. His aide-de-camp Lt. Col. Camille Ferri Pisani wrote about their trip, published by Indiana University Press in 1959 as *Prince Napoleon in America, 1861: Letters from his Aide-de-Camp*, translated with a preface by Georges J. Joyaux, foreword by Bruce Catton, and illustrated by Gil Walker.

1874: Charles Joseph Bonaparte (1851-1921), younger son of brother Jerome "Bo" Bonaparte, graduates from Harvard Law, becomes friends with Theodore Roosevelt, and later serves as Secretary of the Navy and US Attorney General. See the chapter, "Descendants of Jerome and Elizabeth," *The Bonapartes in America* by Macartney & Dorrance, 1939. Also see the six-page fold-out family tree in *The Bonapartes* by David Stacton, 1966. According to Stacton, the America Bonaparte line, at the time of his book's publication, included four living descendants in the female line.

1894: *McClure's Magazine* publishes the first installment of Ida M. Tarbell's Napoleon Bonaparte in the November issue. A Great Pictorial Life of Napoleon with nearly 200 illustrations, says a promotional message across the top of the cover of the 15 cent publication. The collection of articles, heavily illustrated from the collection of Gardiner G. Hubbard, appears two years later as a 248-page section (at the beginning of the volume) in *McClure's Biographies: Napoleon, Gladstone, Bismarck, Grant, Dana, Stevenson and Others*, (New York: The S. S. McClure Co.), 1896.

1894: *The Century Magazine* publishes the first installment of its Napoleon series – also in November – by William M. Sloane. An advertisement (ironically, appearing in the November issue of *McClure's*), says, "The interest in Napoleon has recently had a revival that is phenomenal in its extend and intensity – as evidenced in a flood of publications, in the preparations of works of art dealing with the period, in the demand for autographs and relics of all kinds." The six-part series is heavily illustrated and the annual subscription for *The Century* is $4. According to the Century ad, "No one could have so fine a perspective or be more dispassionate in his judgments than a competent American writer. This new Life of Napoleon is most important and timely because of the abundant materials furnished by the opening of the different national archives, and by the recent publication of valuable memoirs."

1894: Herbert H. Sargent, a first lieutenant in the Second Cavalry stationed at Fort Bowie, Arizona, puts the final touches on his first book. *Napoleon Bonaparte's First Campaign With Comments* is published by A. C. McClurg and Company of Chicago.

1900: *L'Aiglon: A Play in Six Acts* by Edmond Rostand, translated by Louis N. Parker, is performed at the Knickerbocker Theatre in New York City during the month of October, 1900, about Napoleon II, covering the final years of the young Duke's life. The 262-page play was published in New York by R. H. Russell.

1903: The Napoleon Company begins, headquartered in Seattle, Washington. Initially named A. Magnano, the company established 'Napoleon' as their brand in 1907, and in 1960, what was by then called A. Magnano & Sons adopted its current name. The company has, and continues to use images of Napoleon in their packaging: www.napoleon-co.com.

1907: The film "Napoleon & Empress Josephine of France" is released (director James Stuart Blackton).

1911: The Instructor Literature Series brings out the 31-page *Story of Napoleon: The Hero of the French* by Bertha E. Bush, published by the F. A. Owen Publishing Company of Dansville, New York. This is No. 188C in the series, one of 350 volumes in limp cloth.

1913: *The Mentor*, a weekly publication, came out with an issue on Napoleon by its Department of Biography on November 3 (Vol. 1, No. 38) featuring the 11-page "Napoleon Bonaparte" by Ida M. Tarbell, author of *Short Life of Napoleon Bonaparte* and *He Knew Lincoln*. Included in the publication were six suitable-for-framing black & white prints: Napoleon at Arcole by Antoine Jean Gros, Friedland 1807 by Meissonier, Napoleon at St. Helena by Paul Delaroche, Retreat from Moscow by Meissonier, Napoleon On Board the Bellerophon by W. Q. Orchardson, and Emperor Napoleon by Francois Gerard. On the back of each photogravure is information about the historical event portrayed – one for each day of the week, identified from Monday through Saturday. The Mentor Association – an institution of learning established for the development of a popular interest in art, literature, science, history, nature, and travel – was led by an Advisory Board with John G. Hibben, president of Princeton University; Hamilton W. Mabie, author and editor; John C. Van Dyke, professor of History of Art, Rutgers College; Albert Bushnell Hart, professor of Government, Harvard University; William T. Hornaday, director, New York Zoological Park; and Dwight L. Elmendorf, lecturer and traveler. The association's motto was "Learn one thing every day" (inside front cover).

1914: The film "The Man of Destiny" is released, directed by Edwin starring W. Humphrey.

1920s: The Little Leather Library Corporation of New York publishes *Uses of Great Men* by Emerson, including three chapters of the original work: the introduction, Shakespeare and Napoleon; or The Man of the World. The chapter on Napoleon is on pages 77-116.

1923: The Little Blue Book series, edited by E. Haldeman-Julius, brings out *Life of Napoleon* by Charles J. Finger as a 64-page booklet in the Ten Cent Pocket Series (No. 141). Other Napoleonic titles published by the Girard, Kansas, publishers included *Maxims of Napoleon* (No. 155) and *The Empire of Napoleon* by Louis R. Gottschalk (Ph.D., University of Louisville), as No. 878.

1928: The film "Napoleon's Barber" by director John Ford, starring Otto Matiesen is released.

1929: Metro-Goldwyn-Mayer (MGM Studios) releases an abridged version of Abel Gance's "Napoleon," which falls short at the box office (see the chapter "Defeat in America," in Napoleon: Abel Gance's Classic Film by Kevin Brownlow, 1983. Read the Turner Classic Movies review by Brian Cady:
http://www.tcm.com/thismonth/article/88902%7C0/Napoleon

1932: The J. B. Lippincott Company edition of Hilaire Belloc's *Napoleon* has, as the frontpiece, an illustration showing the bust of Napoleon by Ceracchi, "formerly in the possession of Thomas

Jefferson, now owned by Harold J. Coolidge, Esq., Boston, U.S.A." Ceracchi, a Corsican working in Rome, made the bust during the Italian campaign.

1935: Courvoisier (pronounced Kor-vwa-zee-a), 'the brandy of Napoleon,' runs its first full-page ad in *The New Yorker* that would continue for many decades.

1937: "Conquest" is released by MGM, about Napoleon and Polish countess Marie Walewska, directed by Clarence Brown and starring Charles Boyer as Napoleon and Greta Garbo as Marie. The film, "a lavish period drama," is based on the novel by Waclaw Gasiorowski with original music by Herbert Stothart. Boyer received an Academy Award nomination for this role. Read the Turner Classic Movie review by Genevieve McGillicuddy:
http://www.tcm.com/thismonth/article/87781%7C0/Conquest

1939: *The Pittsburgh Press* features a full-page article, "Napoleon's Last Days," on April 30, in preparation of the 118-year anniversary of his death. The article includes photos of current-day St. Helena.

1942: The film "You Were Never Lovier" with Fred Astaire and Rita Haworth includes a reference to a book of Napoleon's love letters.

1946: Francis Coppola's film "It's a Wonderful Life," featuring James Stewart and Donna Reed, includes a prominent bust of Napoleon in the office of the evil Mr. Potter, while a portrait of Abraham Lincoln adorns the offices of Bailey Savings & Loan, the good guys. James Stewart runs up to Potter's window and yells, "Merry Christmas, Mr. Potter" following his encounter with the angel Clarence as he heads home to his friends and family who await him. See the photo in *The It's a Wonderful Life Book*, by Jeanine Basinger, in collaboration with the Trustees of the Frank Capra Archives, interviews by Leonard Maltin, New York: Alfred A. Knopf, 1986, p. 314.

1953: Random House Landmark Books brings out *Napoleon and the Battle of Waterloo* by Frances Winwar and illustrated by David Stone, which becomes the introduction for thousands of elementary-age students to Napoleon. The 183-page book has at least four printings.

1954: The film "Desiree" is released, directed by Henry Koster with Marlon Brando as Napoleon and Jean Simmons.

1965: *Life* magazine's cover story for June 11 was "Waterloo," the great battle 150 years ago; move by move – how the victory hung in the balance, written by Thomas N. Carmichael. The cover art was the famous painting of a British infantry in a square formation defending against French cavalry ("Quatre Bras" by Lady Butler from the National Gallery of Victoria, Melbourne). Of the many reproductions illustrating the 26-page feature, only one came from America ("Napoleon Returns from Elba" by Steube, Calvin Bullock Collection, New York). Introducing Carmichael's story in a page 3 editor's note, Managing Editor George P. Hunt wrote that Carmichael, his administrative assistant, "has been a Waterloo buff since his toy soldier days...Tom sold us on the idea more than a year ago, and Correspondent Kenneth Gouldthorpe of our Paris bureau went to work scouring Europe for paintings of Waterloo. Quoting Carmichael in his introduction, Hunt writes that the article's author told him, "What really interests me is the character, personality and right-or-wrong decisions of the great commanders" (p. 3).

1968-1969: Stanley Kubrick (1928-1999) spends two years planning his movie on Napoleon. Production notes dated November 1968 reference Professor Felix Markham as principal historical advisor and a library of 500 books is assembled. A screenplay totaling 148 pages is dated September 1969. MGM, however, decided not to make the film. A massive book about the project was published in limited edition in 2009, *Stanley Kubrick's Napoleon: The Greatest Movie Never Made* edited by Alison Castle and published by Taschen America. A smaller, more affordable, edition came out in 2011. See www.taschen.com and *New York Magazine*, "The Cinemascope Spectacular of Books" by Tobias Grey, Nov. 29, 2009.

1969. "The Taste of Napoleon: A Loan Exhibition" is sponsored by the Society of Fellows, William Rockhill Nelson Gallery of Art, and the Mary Atkins Museum of Fine Arts (October 2 to November 16) in Kansas City, Missouri. The exhibit publication is the 112 page The Nelson Gallery and Atkins Museum Bulletin, Vol. IV, No. 10, with an introduction by Lincoln Kirstein, who writes: "It does seem that

Napoleon had a passion for a single painting, Albrecht Altdorfer's extremely complicated, panoramic miniature "The Battle of Alexander," which shows hosts of men engaged in a gigantic struggle under stormy skies," p. 30. The exhibit, arranged and the catalogue prepared and edited by Ross E. Taggart, featured source material and books, paintings, sculpture, drawings, prints, furniture, silver, gilt bronze, porcelain and glass, textiles, wall paper and paper, and miscellaneous items including arms and armor, medals, decorations, and jewelry. Among the lenders to the exhibition are these U.S. galleries, museums, libraries, and societies: The Achenbach Foundation for Graphic Arts, California Palace of the Legion of Honor, San Francisco; The Art Institute of Chicago; The Anne S. K. Brown Military Collection, Providence, Rhode Island; The Cincinnati Art Museum; The Sterling and Francine Clark Art Institute, Williamstown, Massachusetts; The Cleveland Museum of Art; The Cooper-Hewitt Museum of Design, Smithsonian Institution; The Detroit Institute of Arts; The Fine Arts Gallery, San Diego; The Fogg Art Museum, Harvard University; The Linda Hall Library, Kansas City, Missouri; The Library of Congress; The Los Angeles County Museum of Art; The Metropolitan Museum of Art; The Minneapolis Institute of Art; The Museum of Fine Arts, Boston; University of Kansas Museum of Art, Lawrence; The Walker Art Center, Minneapolis; The West Point Museum; The Western Reserve Historical Society, Cleveland, Ohio.

1970: "Waterloo," a Mosfilm/Paramount movie, stars Rod Steiger as Napoleon and Christopher Plummer as Wellington. According to one review, the film "required more planning, perhaps, than the battle itself."

1978: The Leslie H. Kuehner Napoleon Collection is donated to the Plough Library at Christian Brothers University consisting of 1,300 books (and sculptures and other memorabilia). Kuehner (1893-1980) lived in Memphis and was manager of the Catholic Club and president of the Particular Council of Memphis of the St. Vincent de Paul Society. He began his collection in 1904 and gave public lecture on Napoleon, which included "America's Debt to Napoleon" and "Napoleon's Love Life."
www.cbu.edu/cbu/Library/Archives/napoleon/index.htm.

1981: A new version of the Abel Gance silent film "Napoleon" for U.S. audiences is set to live music at Radio City Music Hall in New York, written and conducted by Carmine Coppola. A crowd of 6,000 attended the premiere, featuring a 60-piece orchestra for the four and a half-hour film, held over for two weekends and praised by reviewers. "Napoleon took New York by storm," says Kevin Brownlow in his 1983 book about the film. "The Napoleon bandwagon rolled across the United States…bringing the name of Gance to thousands who had never heard of it before," as the film played in 16 cities, ending in Los Angeles (pp. 250-253).

1982: *National Geographic's* cover story for the February issue (Vol. 161, No. 2) was a 47-page article on Napoleon by John J. Putman, National Geographic senior writer with photographs by Gordon W. Gahan, *National Geographic* photographer. Putman and Gahan went on a four-month journey retracing Napoleon's footsteps: "In time I would begin to feel his presence," wrote Putman. "When I arrived someplace, it often seemed as if he had only just departed; the map case, the portable field bed, the cheap snuff he favored all having been shoved hurriedly into an army wagon moments before it clattered off. And I would come to feel I knew the people who had touched his life…" (p. 150). Accompanying a photo of a women looking out of a window from the inside is this caption: "Sign of an emperor, the N on a frosty pane in Czechoslovakia calls to mind a family story told by this retired seamstress, holding her father's picture. One of her ancestors fought with Napoleon at nearby Austerlitz and then, with a French bride, began a humble dynasty of smiths and farmers in a foreign land" (p. 165).

1989-1990: The Phoenix Art Museum exhibits Napoleon the Great: Selections from The David Markham Collection. J. David Markham is president of the International Napoleonic Society, and an author and collector: www.napoleonichistory.com.

1990: Institute on Napoleon and the French Revolution is formally established by Dr. Donald D. Howard at the Department of History, Florida State University, as the only graduate program in the U.S. devoted solely to the study of the Revolutionary and Napoleonic era: www.fsu.edu/napoleon.

1995: The Napoleon Series web site is founded by Fons Libert and Robert Burnham, a retired US Army officer, currently serves as editor-in-chief: www.napoleon-series.org.

1996: The Napoleonic Literature web site was established and its editor is John Schneider, US Army retired master sergeant: www.napoleonic-literature.com.

1996: Michael J. Fox stars in the political sit-com Spin City about the New York City mayor's office – his office as deputy mayor (playing Mike Flaherty) includes a framed print of David's Napoleon Crossing the Alps. The show ran through 2000.

1996: The magazine *Napoleon* begins publication in January by the Emperor's Press of Chicago, with six issues a year, with Dana F. Lombardy as publisher, Jean A. Lochet as chief historian and editor-in-chief, and Matt DeLaMater as managing editor. *Napoleon* switched to a quarterly journal format in 1998 with the sub-title: International Journal of the French Revolution and Age of Napoleon. A total of 17 numbers came out before it ceased publication in 2000. Among the American historians featured in the publication's interview feature were (with the number of that issue): Proctor Patterson Jones (No. 1), Harold T. Parker (No. 7), Col. John Elting (No. 10), Donald Horward (No. 11), Owen Connelly (No. 12), and Gunther Rothenberg (No. 14).

1998: An art review, "A Balance of Naughty and Nice," by Holland Cotter is featured in the March 13 *The New York Times* Fine Arts and Leisure department of the Weekend section, about a survey of the work of Pierre-Paul Prud'hon (1758-1823) at the Metropolitan Museum of Art. The piece includes more than a half-page portrait of Josephine. "His portrait of her, painted around 1805 and set at Malmaison, may be his best-known work, and it is a beauty," writes Cotter. "He tried out many poses for it – Josephine reclining, sitting sideways with legs crossed – before he settled on the final image, in which she leans back on a stone bench, lost in thought, her fingers casually toying with the fillet in her hair."

1998: Napoleonica auction, sold to benefit the Western Reserve

Historical Society – a collection of books, paintings, furniture, decorative arts and militaria, with estimates ranging from $300 to $35,000 – at Christie's East in New York City.

1998: Paula Deitz writes "A Conqueror Captured in His Final Moments," in the Arts/Artifacts section of the July 12 *New York Times* Sunday edition. She wrote about an 1821 drawing in graphite and gray wash on light brown wove paper, "Death Portrait of Napoleon." British artist Joseph William Rubidage made the sketch and an engraving was struck by Henry Hoppner Meyer in London. Always in private hands, the drawing was exhibited at the International Fine Art and Antique Dealers Show in Manhattan the previous fall and later at the private gallery of David and Constance Yates, dealers in European drawings and sculpture, also in Manhattan. "The re-emergence of the drawing sheds light on an aspect of collecting largely beyond public view," writes Deitz. "Because many famous artworks are in private hands, museum collections represent only a portion of the world's treasures."

2000: The Learning Channel (TLC) runs a full-page ad in the April 23 *New York Times* for its world premiere that night of "Napoleon's Obsession: Quest for Egypt." Under the heading, Napoleon Complex, Complex Napoleon, is promotional copy saying "TLC reveals the bizarre secrets of a power-crazed leader during a tumultuous year that would change the world."

2000: Ted Loos writes "A Biography of Presidents Tackles an Emperor," in the November 5 *New York Times* about documentary filmmaker David Grubin's PBS miniseries on Napoleon. "Napoleon is compelling because it is one of the great stories of history," Grubin said. "It's got all the elements of a great romance and a great epic. You couldn't dream it up," he told Loos. The four-hour series, narrated by historian David McCullough, took three years and cost $3 million.

2001-2002: The exhibit, "From Gutenberg to Gone with the Wind: Treasures from the Ransom Center," The University of Texas at Austin, includes an 1812 document signed by Napoleon that confers the Legion of Honor on Camille Frederic Gaulieu.

2003: New Orleans Museum of Art presents "Jefferson's America & Napoleon's France: An Exhibition for the Louisiana Purchase Bicentennial." The 286-page book about the exhibit, in association with University of Washington Press: Seattle & London, features curator for the exhibition committee Gail Feigenbaum, associate director at the Getty Research Institute, with essays by Victoria Cooke (also editor for the book), Patrice Higonnet, Bill Mercer, David O'Brien, Jessie Poesch, Paul Staiti, Susan R. Stein, Paul Tarver, and Susan Taylor-Leduc.

2004: Christie's, New York, presented the House Sale of the "Dr. Philip F. Corso Napoleonic Collection" (December 2), with an introduction by Peter Hicks, historian at the Foundation Napoleon. The 76-page publication includes prints, sculptures, documents, books, signed letters, medals, medallions, and other collectables. "Philip Corso has been a lifelong Napoleon enthusiast," says Hicks. "He fell under the charm about forty years ago after reading Felix Markham's influential 1963 biography, *Napoleon*...Corso's collecting philosophy was always one of eclecticism. So in addition to the prints and caricatures, there are bronze and marble statues, jewelry, china, snuff-boxes, and ultimately a large conglomeration of memorabilia with a Napoleonic theme decoration, such as spoons, pipes and Dalton mugs" (p. 3). At the back of the program is a full-page ad for the Trafalgar Bicentenary: The Age of Nelson, Wellington and Napoleon scheduled for Oct. 19, 2005, at the Christie's location in London. The image of Napoleon in this ad is by Andrea Appiani (1754-1817), "Portrait of Napoleon Bonaparte as First Consul, oil on canvas, 39 x 31¾ in., sold for $769,100 at Christie's New York, June 17, 2004.

2005: *The New York Times* runs more than a half-page color illustration (June 26) of Jacques-Louis David's The Emperor Napoleon in His Study at the Tuileries in "Life is Short, but Good Publicity Lasts Forever," by Annette Grant. The article was about the Jaques-Louis David: Empire to Exile exhibit at the Sterling and Francine Clark Art Institute in Williamstown, Mass.

2005: The New York Public Library, Humanities and Social Sciences Library presents the exhibit "Decoration in the Age of Napoleon:

Empire Elegance Versus Regency Refinement" (September 3 – April 2) in the Edna Barnes Salomon Room. Paula A. Baxter, curator, Art & Architecture Collection, Miriam and Ira D. Wallach Division of Art, Prints and Photographs. The 8-page program includes suggested reading, and the portion for The Empire Style lists: Empire Style 1804-1815 by Nietta Apra (1973), Empire Style by Francois Baudot (1999), Empire by Madeleine Deschamps (2004), The French Empire Style by Alvar Gonzales-Palacio (1970), Empire Furniture, 1800 to 1825 by Serge Grandjean (1966), and L'Empire by Guillaume Janneau (1965).

2005: The Russell Etling Company presents the traveling exhibit "Napoleon: An Intimate Portrait," featuring more than 250 items at locations throughout the U.S., from the collection of Pierre-Jean Chalencon, President, Cercle France-Napoleon. According to the 108-page program of the same name, the exhibition is dedicated to the memory of Robert M. Snibbe, founder of the Napoleonic Society of America. Russell Etling, president of the sponsoring company, writes in the introduction that with the 200th anniversary of Napoleon and Josephine's coronation (1804), "we entered a period of renewed interest in this fascinating period and its central figure...Pierre-Jean Chalencon granted permission for our firm to mount an exhibition of his extraordinary collection of art and objects from the period...Though elements of the collection have been loaned for major exhibitions around the world, this is the first time these irreplaceable artifacts have been seen in our continent." According to Pierre-Jean Chalencon, "The pieces in the exhibition have been selected not only for their great beauty and rarity, but also because they allow us to see into the heart of this extraordinary man."

2005: *Napoleon for Dummies* by historian J. David Markham is published. Don't be fooled by the title; this is great biography.

2006: Napoleonic Historical Society, based in Chicago, is created by the combination of The Napoleonic Alliance and The Napoleonic Society of America: napoleonichistoricalsociety.com

2006: *Antiques and The Arts Weekly* (June 30) features the exhibit "Napoleon on the Nile: Soldiers, Artists, and the Rediscovery of

Egypt," at the Dahesh Museum of Art in New York City. According to the non-bylined story, curator Lisa Small "has selected letters, medals, decorative arts, drawings, watercolors, paintings, illustrated books, prints and photographs from the Brier Collection to complement the museum's own holdings to fully convey Europe's visual imaginings of Egypt between Napoleon's ill-fated invasion and the start of World War I."

2006: Breguet watch ad continues running in the *New Yorker* magazine, show the painting of Napoleon with the caption, "Napoleon Bonaparte, from 1798, a client of Breguet's.

2007: National Public Radio airs an interview with Thomas Venning, director of Books & Manuscripts at Christie's, about a collection of 1,000 documents including a love letter written by Napoleon.

2007: American Federation of Arts produces an online resource for educators, *Symbols of Power: Napoleon and the Art of the Empire Style, 1800-1815,* "to assist you in teaching your students about Napoleon Bonaparte's life and the decorative arts style that he inspired and that flourished under his patronage," p. 4. The guide complemented a national tour made possible, in part, by the Joseph and Sylvia Slifka Foundation, Inc., and the Samuel H. Kress Foundation, and by the Federal Council on the Arts and the Humanities. The AFA is a nonprofit institution that organizes art exhibitions for presentation in museums around the world, publishes exhibition catalogues, and develops education programs:
http://www.afaweb.org/education/documents/SymbolsofPowerTeacherPacket.pdf

2008: The *Pittsburgh Post-Gazette* runs a color illustration (September 16) of the 19th century painting "1806, Jena" by French artist Jean-Louis-Ernest Meissonier on exhibit at The Frick Art & Historical Center.

2008: Garmin runs a 30-second ad during the Super Bowl for its GPS depicting Napoleon driving to join his troops using their device to find his way, and upon arriving, hiding it in his coat, mimicking his famous hand-in-waist coat pose. It's worth watching; Google it.

2009: *The Wall Street Journal* runs an article (June 11), "Napoleon and America," by Julia M. Klein in the Leisure & Arts section on the exhibit in Philadelphia featuring the collection of Pierre-Jean Chalencon. Klein is a cultural reporter and critic in Philadelphia and a contributing editor at Columbia Journalism *Review*.

2009: The first English edition of "The Eagle and the Lion" comes out, a strategy game in the Battles of Napoleon series by Ugo Di Meglio and Sergio Guerri of Italy, "not just one game, but rather a gaming system that enables you to recreate many important battles of this period…based on serious historical research. Well-coordinated use of infantry, cavalry, and artillery, plus skillful maneuvering of your units, and understanding your troop's strengths and weaknesses, are essential…" The boards and gaming pieces are accompanied by a 48-page rules of play and a 24-page booklet of scenarios.

2010: Coca-Cola runs a television spot featuring Napoleon and other historical figures to help a history student preparing for an exam (shades of Bill & Teds Excellent Adventure).

2011: Barrymore Laurence Scherer writes "The Comeback: The National Academy Reopens with Six New Exhibitions," posted Sept. 15 at www.themagazineantiques.com, mentioning that when the New York Academy of the Fine Arts was established in 1802 Napoleon (then First Counsel) was invited to become the first honorary member. He accepted and also sent the Academy a reference library and a collection of Piranesi etchings.

2011: CNN Living section online carries the story "Napoleon's Brother in New Jersey?" by Matt Soniak. (Refer to the 1815 listing for background).

2012: Abe Gance's film Napoleon is featured at the San Francisco Silent Film Festival during March and April in celebration of the U.S premiere of the film. Turner Classic Movies is the official media sponsor. See the promotional trailer on YouTube: http://www.youtube.com/watch?v=v1m5Q09eEqY

8
THE ART OF NAPOLEON

I added this chapter because of the great amount of Napoleonic art available across America, selecting only a handful of museums, art galleries, and a library. The record of the donors of many of these works of art is also noted as another dimension of Napoleon's connection with the American public. While the works of art may not always be on display, the listings mentioned here are pictured on these organization's websites (as of October 2011). Some of the referenced works are currently being exhibited.

Smithsonian American Art Museum
Washington, D.C.
http://americanart.si.edu

George Edwin Bissell (1839-1920), "Napoleon I," after 1875, plaster figurine, gift of John Watts De Peyster.

Solon H. Borglum (1868-1922), "Napoleon at Moscow: The Command of God to Retreat," 1910, bronze, gift of Monica B. Davies and Paul Borglum, 1968.

Henry Brintnell Bounetheau (1797-1877):

- "Napoleon Bonaparte," 1850, watercolor on ivory, copied from a painting of Napoleon crossing the Alps, gift of Mrs. Henry Du Pre Bounetheau, 1946.
- "Napoleon as General," 1847, miniature, watercolor on ivory, copy after Thomas Sully (1783-1872), copy after Andrea Appiani (1754-1817), gift of Mrs. Henry Du Pre, 1946.

Ruth Gikow (1915-1982), "Psychosis – Two Napoleons and a Josephine," n.d., serigraph print, 13¼ x 10 in., gift of Audrey McMahon, 1968.

92

Launt Thompson (1833-1894), "Napoleon I," modeled ca. 1866, full-length bronze sculpture, 73½ x 26 x 23 in., gift of Dr. Gifford B. Pinchot, 1961.

Henry Wolf (1852-1916):

- "Death of Napoleon I," 1896, print, photomechanical wood engraving, 1973.

- "Napoleon as Emperor," 1895, print, wood engraving, 1973.

- "Napoleon Before the Sphinx," 1888, print, wood engraving, 5 x 8¼, 1973.

- "Submission of the Mamelukes to Napoleon," 1895, print, wood engraving, copy after Custave Bourgain (1856-1918), 5 x 7½, 1973.

National Gallery of Art
Washington, D.C.

www.nga.gov

Antoine-Louis Barye (1795-1875), "General Bonaparte on Horseback," model c. 1838, cast after 1847, 14¾ x 13 x 5¼, collection of Mr. & Mrs. Paul Mellon, 1980.

Jacques-Louis David (1748-1825), "The Emperor Napoleon in His Study at the Tuileries,"1812, oil on canvas, 80¼ x 49¼, special website features discussing the painting, plus special features for children, Samuel H. Kress Collection, 1961. Read more about the legacy of Samuel H. Kress at www.kressfoundation.org.

Also see "Five-and-Dime for Millions: The Samuel H. Kress Collection" by Marilyn Perry, *Apollo Magazine*, March 1991 (adapted from a November 1990 symposium paper delivered at the Spencer Museum of University of Kansas for the 30th anniversary of its Kress Study Collection). See also the proceedings from that symposium in the *Register* of the Spencer Museum.

Charles Francois Gabriel Levachez 1760-1820), "Bonaparte Premier Consul de la Republique Francaise," n.d., color aquatint and etching, gift of Mrs. W. Murray Crane, 1954.

Charles Turner (1773-1857), "Bonaparte Reviewing the Consular Guard," n.d., color aquatint, mezzotint, and etching, after John James Masquerier (1778-1855), gift of Mrs. W. Murray Crane, 1954.

The Art Institute of Chicago
www.artic.edu

Dr. C. Francesco Antommarchi, "Death Mask of Napoleon," (from a mold by), modeled 1821, cast 1833, cast by Louis Richard and E. Quesnel.

Francesco Bartolozzi (1727-1815) and Andrea Appiani the Elder (1754-1817), "Napoleon Bonaparte, First Counsel," 1802, engraving and stipple engraving on ivory, 391 x 41 mm., gift of Col. Robert R. McCormack.

Jacques Louis David (1748-1825):

- "Profile of Napoleon," c. 1810, black chalk, with touches of black crayon, 185 x 138 mm., Helen Regenstein Collection, 1961.

- "Study," 1811/12, black chalk with black crayon, 185 x 138 mm., Helen Regenstein Collection, 1961.

Auguste Gaspard Louis Desnoyers (1779-1857), "Napoleon the Great," 1805, after Francois Gerard (1770-1837), engraving, 568 x 415 mm., gift of Mr. & Mrs. Potter Palmer, Jr.

James Ensor (1860-1949), "Napoleon's Farewell," 1897, etching with dry point from a copper plate, 121 x 187 mm., Print & Drawing Purchase Fund, 1968.

Jean Leon Gerome (1824-1904), "Napoleon Entering Cairo," c. 1900, gilt bronze, cast by Siot-Decauville, 15 x 17 in., without base, George F. Harding Collection.

Jean-Baptiste de Grateloup (1735-1817) and Jean Pierre Sylvestre, "Napoleon," n.d., engraving on paper, 29 x 24 mm., 1945.

Eugene L. Lami (1800-1890), "The Translation of the Ashes of Napoleon, 15 December 1840," c. 1842, watercolor and gouache with traces of graphite, 153 x 257 mm., Suzane Dixon Fund, 1986.

Denis Auguste Marie Raffet (1804-1860), "Napoleon in Egypt," 1835, lithograph, 280 x 225 mm., gift of the Print and Drawing Club, 1923.

Henri de Toulouse-Lautrec (1864-1901), "Napoleon," 1895, lithograph, 595 x 463 mm., Albert H. Wolf Fund, 1941.

Unknown artist, "Napoleon," after 1835, after Nicolas Toussaint Charlet (1792-1845), possibly after Denis Auguste Marie Raffet (1804-1860), watercolor and gouache over traces of graphite, 132 x 163 mm., The Charles Deering Collection, 1927.

Unknown artist (French School), "Figure of Napoleon," c. 1820, bronze, 9¼ in. high, gift of Mrs. Laurence Armour, 1964.

The Metropolitan Museum of Art
New York City
www.metmuseum.org.

Jean-Auguste Barre (1811-1896), "Napoleon I," 1838, bronze sculpture, 11 5/16 x 4 5/8 in., gift of Waleed G. Maloff, 1990.

Antoine-Louis Barye (1796-1875), "General Bonaparte in the Uniform of a General," possibly ca. 1838, bronze sculpture, 4 1/8 x 3 in., without base, gift of Dr. Maria A. S. de Reinis, 1978.

Alexis Joseph Depaulis (1790/92-1867), "Napoleon Lying Dead at St. Helena/Commemoration of the Return of Napoleon's Remains to France," 1840, 1840 or later, bronze medal, 2 ½ in., Rogers Fund, 1977.

Alphonse Francois (1814-1888), "Napoleon Crossing the Alps," 1851, after Hippolyte Delaroche (1797-1856), engraving (proof before letters), 24 7/8 x 19 7/16 in., The Elisha Whittelsey Collection, 1949.

Francois Gerard (1770-1837), "Portrait of Napoleon I," designed 1805, woven 1808-1811, tapestry (wool, silk, silver-gilt thread), 87½ x 57½ in., Joseph Pulitzer bequest, 1943.

Dihl et Guerhard (1781-1824), Napoleon Bonaparte as First Consul," ca. 1800, hard-paste biscuit porcelain, 12½ in. high, gift of Countesse Marie-Elizabeth Albert d'Enno, 1991.

Jean Baptiste Isabey (1767-1855):

- "Napoleon I," 1810, ivory, 2 x 1 1/8 in., gift of Junius S. and Henry S. Morgan, 1947.

- "Napoleon I," 1812, ivory, 2¼ x 1 3/8 in., miniature, gift of Helen O. Brice, 1942.

Luigi Marta (1790-1858), "Napoleon I on Horseback," 1830, ivory, miniature, 5¾ x 7½ in., gift of Gloria Zicht, 1992.

Ernest Meissonier (1815-1891), "1807, Friedland," ca. 1861-1875, oil on canvas, 53½ x 95½, gift of Henry Hilton, 1887.

Unknown artist (French painter), "Napoleon Bonaparte," mid-19th century, oil on wood, 8¼ x 15 in., gift of Estate of P. R. Strong, 1877.

Franz Zeichner, "Commemorating Marriage of Napoleon and Marie Louise," 1810, gold, gift of C. Ruxton Love, Jr., 1967.

Philadelphia Museum of Art
www.philamuseum.org

Jean Pierre Droz (1746-1823), "Portrait Medal of Napoleon," 1804, obverse and Andre Galle (1761-1844), reverse after Antoine Denis Chaudet (1763-1810), directed by Baron Dominique Vivant Denon

(1747-1825), silver, 1 inch diameter, bequest of Anthony Morris Clark, 1978.

Andre-Leon Larue (1785-c.1834), attributed to, c. 1810, watercolor on ivory, miniature mounted in a leather portfolio, 4 1/16 x 3 in., gift of Mrs. Jacob Riegel and Mrs. Daniel Whitney, 1952.

Johann Friedrich Wihelm Muller (1782-1816), "Profile Portrait of Napoleon Bonaparte," 1802-1803, etching, engraving and aquatint, 4 5/16 x 3¼ in., gift of Muriel and Philip Berman.

Henri de Toulouse-Lautrec (1864-1901), "Napoleon," 1895, color lithograph, 25 5/16 x 19 in., gift of R. Sturgis and Marion B. F. Ingersoll, 1940.

Friedrich Weber (1813-1882), "Napoleon and His Son," mid-19th century, after Carl von Steuben (1788-1856), etching and engraving, 17 15/16 x 14½ in., gift of Muriel and Philip Berman.

Unknown artist (French), "Napoleon Bonaparte, Proclaimed Emperor of France in Paris, May 20, 1804," hand-colored etching, 10 7/8 x 8 9/16 in., bequest of Henry Reed Hatfield, 1943.

Museum of Fine Arts Boston
www.mfa.org

J. B. J. Duchesne (1770-1856), "Napoleon I," miniature, 2 13/16 x 2 3/16 in., gift of Miss Miriam Shaw.

Conrad Gessner (1764-1826), "Study for Napoleon's Campaign," undated, watercolor, 8 1/8 x 11 15/16 in., gift of Francis Bartlett, 1912.
Horatio Greenough (1805-1852), "Napoleon I," 1847, marble sculpture, 23¼ x 14 x 10¾ , gift of Mrs. Horatio Greenough.

Robert Lefeve (1755-1830), "Portrait of Napoleon I in His Coronation Robes," 1812, oil on canvas, 98 7/8 x 75 3/8 in., gift of William Sturgis Bigelow Collection.

Frederic Millet, "Napoleon I," ivory miniature, 10¼ x 8 3/8 in., gift of John Templeman Coolidge.

Southworth and Hawes, "Painted Portrait of Napoleon," photograph, daguerreotype, 4¼ x 3¼ in., gift of Richard Parker.

Unidentified artist, "Bust of Napoleon I," made by Sevres Manufacturing after Antoine-Denis Chaudet (1763-1810), hard-paste biscuit porcelain, 20 11/16 x 10 5/8, provenance mentions Napoleon as the original owner, gift of Randolph J. Fuller, Mrs. Caleb Loring, John L. Gardner, G. Peabody and Rose Gardner Charitable Trust and Edward Jackson Holmes Fund.

Unidentified artist (American), "Napoleon on Dappled Horse," 19th century, pen and red, blue and dark brown inks on board, 19 ¾ x 16 in., gift of Maxim Karolik for the M. and M. Karolik Collection of American Watercolor & Drawings 1800-1875.

Unidentified artist, hinged oval sable box, full view of Napoleon with a telescope, beadwork with glass beads, gift of Elizabeth Day McCormick Collection.

Unidentified artist, "Napoleon: Veille d' Austerlitz," early 19th century, pen and ink with calligraphy, 10 1/8 x 15 in., gift of Miss Aimee and Miss Rosamond Lamb.

Unidentified artist (French), "Portrait of Napoleon," silk weaving, gift of Mrs. Henry P. Sturgis.

Unidentified artist, "Stone Carved Figure of Napoleon," 1825-1850, limestone, 19 x 6 x 6 in., gift of William E. Nicker.

Other collections

Brooklyn Museum, www.brooklynmuseum.org, "Napoleon Standing with a Soldier," 1831, Joseph-Louis-Hippolyte Bellange (1800-1866), graphite and watercolor on wove paper, 4 5/8 x 3 15/16 in., bequest of Marion Reilly.

Detroit Institute of Arts, www.dia.org, "Dedication of the Napoleon Museum, Paris," Andrieu, not dated, bronze medal with side view of Napoleon, 1 3/8 diameter, gift of A. H. Griffith.

The J. Paul Getty Museum (Los Angeles, California), www.getty.edu/museum, "Napoleon at the Battlefield of Eylau," 1807, attributed to Antoine-Jean Gros (1771-1835), pen and black and dark brown ink over graphite, 10 5/8 x 17 5/8 in.

The Walters Art Museum (Baltimore, Maryland), www.thewalters.org, "1814," 1862, Jean-Louis-Ernest Meissonier (1815-1891), oil on panel, 12 ¾ x 9 ½ in. This scene of Napoleon on horseback was commissioned by Napoleon's nephew Prince Napoleon.

New Orleans Museum of Art, www.noma.org, "Pest House at Jaffa," oil sketch by Baron Gros, 1799, a piece done in advance of a full-scale oil painting. The final work, "Bonaparte Visiting the Plague House at Jaffa," 1804, is in The Louve. According to Art History Professor Noah Charney, this is one of the 10 must-see artworks in New Orleans. "It is a rare treat to find an oil sketch," he says. Also see *Jefferson's America & Napoleon's France: An Exhibition for the Louisiana Purchase Bicentennial*, 2003.

The Frick Collection (New York City), www.frick.org, Photo Archive Collection includes "Napoleon Bonaparte" by an anonymous artist (Austrian School), graphic reproduction with documentation of a pen and ink drawing, 9 7/8 x 8 ½ oval, acquired by Gen. John Armstrong (1758-1843) while serving as U.S. Minister to the Court of Napoleon (1804-1810) "as a memento of his friendly relationship with the Emperor." Original remains in his family's possession.

John Hay Library (Brown University, Providence, Rhode Island), http://library.brown.edu/about/hay/, home of the Anne S. K. Brown Military Collection, featuring photographs of Napoleon's veterans (likely taken in Paris in 1858) along with prints, drawings, and watercolors.

For Further Reading

Albert Boime, *Art in the Age of Bonapartism 1800-1815* (volume two in the A Social History of Modern Art), The University of Chicago Press, 1990.

Molly Cygan and Suzanne Elder Burke, *Symbols of Power: Napoleon and the Art of the Empire Style, 1800-1815*, 39-page online resource for educators by the American Federation of Arts, 2007: http://www.afaweb.org/education/documents/SymbolsofPowerTeacherPacket.pdf

Laban Carrick Hill, *A Brush with Napoleon: An Encounter with Jacques-Louis David*, Art Encounters series, New York: Watson-Guptill, 2007.

Edgar Munhall, "Portraits of Napoleon," *Yale French Studies* issue titled "The Myth of Napoleon," No. 26, Fall-Winter 1960-1961.

For a British perspective, see "Napoleon's Great Cultural Charade," by Alan Forrest, *BBC History Magazine* (Vol. 13, No. 13), 2012, pp. 50-55. References for this article include *After the Revolution: Antoine-Jean Gros, Painting and Propaganda Under Napoleon* by David O'Brien (2006) and *Napoleonic Art: Nationalism and the Spirit of Rebellion in France, 1815-1848* by Barbara-Ann Day-Hickman (1999).

For a listing of museums and galleries cited in Proctor Patterson Jones' lavishly illustrated *Napoleon: An Intimate Account of the Years of Supremacy 1800-1814* (Proctor Jones Publishing: San Francisco, 1992), see his Iconography on page 444. He writes: "I started using only old engravings. I found portraits old enough for the subjects themselves to have seen. One thing led to another until I had secured a broad representation of Napoleonic art treasure."

Napoleonic art is on Facebook (Google "Napoleon in Modern Art" and "Facebook"). The content, all in the public domain according to the site, includes paintings, drawings, prints and sculptures by contemporary artists and appears in a slideshow format.

NOTES

Cover Illustration

Rebecca Sinclair did this drawing, commissioned especially for this book, in charcoal pencil after James Fagan's 1894 lithograph (which is signed 'Jas Fagan' in pencil and is in the possession of the author). Fagan was a New York City painter and etcher whose work appeared in H. H. Bancroft's *Achievements of Civilization: 1896-1905*, and had his works exhibited at the Art Institute of Chicago, the Boston Art Club, and the National Academy of Design.

Jean-Baptiste Greuze's portrait of 22-year-old First Lieutenant Bonaparte is featured in a number of biographies. The image appears as the frontpiece, with the caption "Bonaparte at twenty-two years of age," in Ida M. Tarbell's *A Short Life of Napoleon* (with 250 illustrations from the collection of the Hon. Gardiner G. Hubbard) published in 1896 by The S. S. McClure Co., New York.

The following appears on that page under the caption: "After a portrait by Greuze. This portrait was exhibited at the 'Exposition des portraits du Siecle' at the Ecole des Beaux Arts in 1893: No. 111 – Bonaparte, Lieutenant d'Artillerie – par Greuze, Jean Baptiste. Collection de M. le Marquis de Las Cases." The caption continues: "As this is reputed to be the earliest portrait of Napoleon in existence, Mr. Hubbard wrote to the Marquis de Las Cases asking its history. In September, 1894, he received a letter from which the following is quoted: 'Madame du Colombier had the portrait of Lieutenant Bonaparte painted in 1791 by Greuze, who was going through Valance, and who was then fifty-eight years old. The portrait afterwards passed to Madame de Bressieux, her daughter, and it was only upon the death of Madame de Bressieux, in 1847, that my uncle was able to secure the picture, which was left to me."

The Greuze portrait is also the frontpiece plate (with tissue) of the first volume of the 1885 leather and marble board "new and revised edition" of New York publisher Thomas Y. Crowell & Company's *Memoirs of Napoleon Bonaparte* by Louis Antoine Fauvelet, edited by Colonel R. W. Phipps. There is no title on that plate – just the image – however in the List of Illustrations it is identified only as "Portrait of Napoleon I from the painting by Grueze."

Greuze's portrait appears (although not as the frontpiece) as one of the 16 illustrations in Hilaire Belloc's *Napoleon*, published in 1932 by Philadelphia's J. B. Lippincott Company. The plate carries the caption, "Napoleon aged 22, by Greuze. In the Possession of M. le Marquis de Las Cases. Reputed to be the earliest portrait." Meanwhile, the frontpiece in this volume was the bust of Napoleon by Ceracchi, "formally in the possession of Thomas Jefferson, now owned by Harold J. Coolidge, Esq., Boston USA)."

An engraving of the Greuze work is housed in France at Malmaison and Bois-Preau (Thierry Lentz, *Napoleon: 'My Ambition was Great,'* Discoveries series, Harry N. Abrams, Inc., Publishers, New York: 2004, shown p. 13 with illustration credit p. 153).

1: Napoleon USA

1. William Milligan Sloane, *The Life of Napoleon Bonaparte*, revised edition (New York: The Century Co.), 1912, p. 300 in the chapter titled "Napoleon's Place in History." See also his chapter on "Napoleon and the United States." Sloane taught history at Princeton University when his four-volume study was first published in 1896 and was on the history faculty at Columbia University at the time of this revised edition, the four-volume 'library edition.'

2. Albert Leon Guerard, *Reflections on the Napoleonic Legend* (New York: Charles Scribner's Sons), 1924, pp. 107 and 112 in his chapter "The Fascination of Napoleon." Guerard was born in Paris, but moved to the U.S. in 1906 and was teaching at the Rice Institute when he wrote this. The quote continues with Washington as "the perfect contrast to the great Corsican." For more discussion on comparisons of Napoleon and Washington, see the concluding chapter in Ines Murat

(translated by Frances Frenaye), "The Napoleonic and the American Dreams Face to Face," in *Napoleon and the American Dream* (Baton Rouge: Louisiana State University Press), 1981. Also see the epilogue, "In Search of Bonaparte," in Philip Dwyer's *Napoleon: The Path to Power* (New Haven: Yale University Press), 2008. He asks, discussing a general like Bonaparte coming to power in France, "Why not a general like Washington? This is where the role of the individual in history comes into play" (p. 519).

3. *Vanity Fair*, March 2012, p. 369. Includes a photograph of Kevin Brownlow by Emma Hardy. *The New York Times*, Arts & Leisure section, with full-page continuation on p. 13. A photo of Abel Gance in 1967 with Kevin Brownlow says how Brownlow became interested in Gance's Napoleon as a teenager. For a complete history of the film see *Napoleon: Abel Gance's Classic Film* by Kevin Brownlow (with research collaborators Bambi Ballard, Veronica Bamfield, Lenny Borger, and Bernard Eisenchitz), Alfred A. Knopf, New York, 1983. For background on the Stanley Kubrick plans for a Napoleon film, see the Chronology chapter for 1968-1969.

4. Pawn Stars: Travis Benton, e-mail, May 7, 2012.

5. Antiques Road Show, see their archives at www.pbs.org/wgbh/roadshow/archive. The Andrew Brunk interview was accessed on January 24, 2012.

6. Google "Napoleon on Horseback" and "Decorative Arts" and you will find more than 40,000 hits. A 25-inch bronze statuette by Louis-Marie Morise (1818-1883) sold for $20,000. Jon Meacham, *Thomas Jefferson: The Art of Power* (New York: Random House), 2012, p. 448. His note section for a description of the parlor cites: www.monticello.org/site/house-and-gardens/parlor.

7. Napoleon Company, read more at www.napoleon-co.com. Also see J. David Markham, *Napoleon for Dummies* (Indianapolis, Indiana: Wiley Publishing), 2005, for many interesting observations.

8. For alternate history, also see *The Napoleon Options: Alternative Decisions of the Napoleonic Wars* edited by Jonathan North

(Mechanicsburg: Pennsylvania), 2000. In the introduction, North writes that the book "...belongs to a strong if neglected genre and follows in the footsteps of a number of enriching images of world history as it might have been...our aim is to present historical scenarios very firmly rooted in historical reality – this is not fiction, but simulated fact" (pp. 9-10). Chapter authors are Paddy Griffith, Charles S. Grant, Philip Haythornthwaite, John H. Gill, Digby Smith, Jonathan North, John G. Gallaher, Peter Hofschroer, Andrew Uffindell, and Colonel John R. Elting. David A. Bell, while he was teaching history at Johns Hopkins University, wrote in his *The First Total War: Napoleon's Europe and the Birth of Warfare As We Know It* (in the chapter, "The Lure of the Eagle") asks the question of how history would have remembered Napoleon had he died earlier than he did, like in battle or from one of the several assassination attempts. "Of course, counterfactual speculation of this sort always has a parlor-game feel to it, but in this case, it reveals a great deal about both Napoleon and the beginnings of total warfare..." (p. 186). I have always thought that an interesting alternate history thesis for consideration would be to follow through with the question: would WWI and WWII have occurred if Napoleon had succeeded in creating European alliances?

9. Bill Truettner, phone interview, Dec. 6, 2011. He has served in his post since 1965. The collage by Joseph Cornell (1903-1972) is untitled and undated, but consists of a woman in crocheted vest, painting of Napoleon, and a dressmaker's mannequin, done with stain on wood panel 10 1/8 x 8 in., a gift of the Joseph and Robert Cornell Memorial Foundation. According to the museum's website, Cornell is "one of America's most innovative artists" and was "a premier assemblagist, who elevated the box to a major art form."

10. R.S. Alexander, *Napoleon*, in the Arnold 'Reputations' series (New York: Oxford University Press), 2001, p. 163-164.

11. Napoleon, Michigan: Township History, compiled by Ed Barber (1917) and Wayne Russler (2001), Research Center of the Jackson County Library: www.napoleontownship.us/history and www.napoleonmichigan.com.

12. Read about the Grand Hotel on Mackinac Island: http://grandhotel.com/mobile-accommodations/mobile-named-suites

13. City of Kalamazoo, "City Hall" brochure, John Urschel, Records & Information Manager, City Clerk's Office, Division of Records Management, Research and Archives, no date.

14. Phillip J. Pirages, "Selections from the Rare Book Collection at Kalamazoo College," p. 28, in *The Legacy of Albert May Todd*, edited by Joseph S. Czestochowski, published by the Kalamazoo Historic Conservancy for the Preservation of Art, 2000. This beautiful, 181-page volume, was published for the sesquicentennial of the birth of A. M. Todd with grants from the Monroe-Brown Foundation, Irving S. Gilmore Foundation, A. M. Todd Company Foundation, Dorothy U. Dalton Foundation, and KALSEC Incorporated Foundation. In addition to Pirages' piece and one on the legacy of A. M. Todd by the editor, perspectives of Todd's art collection are provided by Michael Quick and Gabriel P. Weisberg. Historical perspectives are provided by Susan C. Brown, Ian Blair, Suzanne Todd Shepard, Paul H. Todd, Jr., Patrick Norris, and Tom Thinnes. Also included is an undated lecture by A. M. Todd, titled "Copy of Some Rough Notes Hastily Written at the Request of the Ladies' Club of Mendon Describing Some of the Objects in my Art Museum & Library" (Mendon is a town near Kalamazoo). Read about the Rare Book Room at: www.kzoo.edu/is/library/rarebook/index.html.

15. Western Michigan University, Mindi K. Bagnell, e-mail, March 6, 2008.

16. Ball State University, "What Middletown Read," see: http://www.bsu.edu/libraries/wmr/. See also the essay by Anne Trubeck, "What Muncie Read," *New York Times Book Review*, November 27, 2011. Other books circulated during this time by Muncie patrons were: *The History of Napoleon Buonaparte* by Lockhart, *The Conscript: A Story of the French War 1813* by Emile Erckmann, *The Imperial Guard of Napoleon: From Marengo to Waterloo* by Headley, *History of the Expedition to Russia* by Philippe-Paul Seur, *Napoleon in Exile* (also titled *A Voice from St. Helena*) by Barry O'Meara, *Historical and Secret*

Memoirs of the Empress Josephine by M. A. Le Normand, *Napoleon: The Last Phase* by Earl of Rosebery, and these titles by Imbert Saint-Amand: *Marie Louise: The Island of Elba & The Hundred Days, Citizeness Bonaparte: The Court of the Empress Josephine, The Wife of the First Counsel, The Happy Days of the Empress Marie Louise.*

17. Albert Leon Guerard, *Reflections on the Napoleonic Legend* (New York: Charles Scribner's Sons), 1924, p. 101, in the chapter titled "The Fascination of Napoleon."

18. David A. Bell, "Just Like Us," The New Republic, May 17, 2004, pp. 34-37 (his review of Steven Englund's *Napoleon: A Political Life*). Read more about Dr. Bell at his website: www.davidavrombell.com.

2: The Faint Echo

1. Ralph Waldo Emerson, "Napoleon; or The Man of the World," in *Representative Men*, 1850, available as an e-text with notes by Frank Davidson, Professor of English, Indiana University (published in Indiana University Publications, Humanities Series No. 16, 1947) at the Reading Room site of napoleon.org that prints out as 21 pages. It is also interesting to note that the Little Leather Library Corporation, New York, edition of Emerson's *Uses of Great Men* (no date, but from the 1920s) has just three of the chapters, the introduction followed by the chapters on Shakespeare and Napoleon within the 116 page condensed version.

2. Paul Fregosi, *Dreams of Empire: Napoleon and the First World War 1792-1815* (NY: Birch Lane Press Book), 1990, p. 23.

3. R. S. Alexander, *Napoleon* (NY: Oxford University Press), 2001, pp. 162-164.

4. A survey of American publishers issuing Napoleonic memoirs includes: E. L. Carey and A. Hart of Philadelphia (Caulincourt's *Napoleon and His Times*, 1838), Thomas Crowell & Co., of New York (Bourrienne's four volume *Memoirs of Napoleon Bonaparte*, edited by R. W. Phipps, 1885), several titles from D. Appleton & Co., of New York (D'Abrantes 'Madame Junot' *Memoirs of Napoleon: His Court and*

Family, 1895, Meneval's three volume *Memoirs Illustrating the History of Napoleon: 1802-1815* edited by his grandson Baron Napoleon Joseph de Meneval,1895, Count de Segur's *An Aide-de-Camp of Napoleon*, revised by his grandson Count Louis de Segur,1897, Lady Mary Loyd's *New Letters of Napoleon I: Omitted from the Edition Published Under the Auspices of Napoleon III from the French*,1897), Merriam Company (Constant's three-volume *Recollections of The Private Life of Napoleon* translated by Walter Clark, 1895), C. M. Saxton, Barker & Co., of New York (Lockhart's *Life of Napoleon Bonaparte*, 1860), and Charles Scribner's Sons of New York (de Bourrienne's four-volume *Memoirs of Napoleon Bonaparte* edited by R. W. Phipps, 1891).

5. A sampling of other writers not included in this study due to the limited scope of their treatment (in chronological order): Ralph Waldo Emerson (18-page chapter "Napoleon: Man of the World" in *Representative Men*, 1850); an anonymous title of 422 pages from John E. Potter and Company (*Napoleon and His Campaigns*, n.d., but sometime before 1851); Henry Watson's 448-page school text (*The Campfires of Napoleon*, 1854) is cited in Dodge's sources; Rufus W. Griswold, the editor of a popular poetry anthology that made the best-seller list in 1842, was the anonymous author of this 720 page collective biography (*Napoleon and His Marshals of the Empire*, Philadelphia: Henry T. Coates,1885, two volumes in one with the binder's title of *Napoleon and His Marshals*); the noted travel writer and lecturer John L. Stoddard's 260-page pictorial biography (*Napoleon: From Corsica to St. Helena*, Akron, Ohio: Saalfield Publishing, 1900 with 1894 copyright); and Montgomery B. Gibbs' 514-page book, cited in Dodge's sources and dedicated to John L. Stoddard. (*Military Career of Napoleon the Great*, Akron, Ohio: Saalfield Publishing, 1902 with 1895 copyright, with binder's title of *Napoleon's Military Career*).

6. Headley, J. T., *Napoleon and His Marshals* (New York: Baker and Scribner), 1847. This version is identified as the 10th edition. At the end of the volume are advertisements for books, including five pages of testimonials for this volume including comments from the *Detroit Free Press, New York Tribune, New Jersey Journal, Cincinnati Chronicle, Pennsylvanian, Columbia Chronicle* (South Carolina) *Chronicle, Lafayette Courier* (Indiana), *Madison Advocate* (Wisconsin), and the *Teacher's Advocate* (Syracuse). His book, *The Imperial Guard of Napoleon*, (New

York: Charles Scribner, 1851) was identified on the binding as *The Old Guard of Napoleon*. In his introduction to this work, Headley explains that the majority of the material was left over from his research for this two-volume history of *Napoleon and His Marshals* and that "The present work lays no claim to originality." This 1851 volume referenced only one source, a French history of the *Imperial Guard* by Emile Marco de Saint Hiliare. This edition, like the two-volumes on the marshals, was available in its entirety on the Napoleonic Literature web site. Regarding the availability of the book in 1923 by Haldeman-Julius Company, see the note in the bibliography of Charles J. Finger, *Life of Napoleon*, Little Blue Book No. 141 (Girard, Kansas: Haldeman-Julius), 1923. The Little Blue Books were also known as the Ten Cent Pocket Series.

7. Headley, Ibid, Preface, Vol. I, pp. i-viii, with references to pp. iv and viii. Richard B. Morris, editor, *Encyclopaedia of American History* (NY: Harper & Brothers, 1953), mentions that not only was *Napoleon and His Marshals* a best-seller in 1846, but that it continued to be a best-seller "after their period, including cheap reprints." p. 566.

8. *New Englander & Yale Review* (October 1846, Vol. 4, Issue 16), pp. 592-594.

9. Connelly, Owen and Scott, Jesse, "Joel T. Headley," *Dictionary of Literary Biography: American Historians 1607-1865*, edited by Clyde N. Wilson, (Detroit: Bruccoli Clark Books/Gale Research Company), 1984, pp. 109-110.

10. Kunitz, Stanley J. and Haycraft, Howard, *American Authors: 1600-1900* (New York: H. W. Wilson Co.), 1938, p. 353.

11. Napoleonic Literature (http://www.napoleonic-literature.com/), posted in October 1998, using the 1850 edition by New York based Hurst & Company.

12. Abbot, John S. C., *The History of Napoleon Bonaparte* (New York: Harper & Brothers), 1883.

13. Kunitz, p. 2.

14. Abbott, iii-iv.

15. Kunitz, p. 2.

16. Andrews, George Gordon, *Napoleon in Review* (New York: Alfred A. Knopf), 1939, p. 306.

17. Kunitz, p. 3.

18. Published as an on-demand book in September 2002, by Indypublish.com in both paper and hard cover. There are also excerpts available online from the *Harper's Magazine* serialization of his biography from Project Gutenberg E-Text released in February 2003, Gutenberg Literary Archive Foundation produced by Brett Fishburneat: http://wwwonlinebooks.library.upenn.edu/webbin/gutbook/lookup ?num 3775.

19. Kunitz, p. 661.

20. Ropes, John Codman, *The First Napoleon: A Sketch, Political & Military* (Boston: Houghton Mifflin), 1885, pp. iii and vi.

21. http:/www.napoleonic-literature.com.

22. Sloane, William Milligan, *Life of Napoleon Bonaparte* (New York: Century Company), 1912 (copyright 1896, Library Edition, four volumes, revised and enlarged with portraits), Vol. 1, p. vi.

23. Ibid., Vol. 4, p. 305.

24. See Appendix A: Chandler (*Campaigns*), p. 9; Bourne, p. 747; and Guerard (*Napoleon*), p. 195; and Guerard (*Reflections*), p. 178.

25. John Schneider, introduction to the CD edition of Sloane's work: http://www.napoleonic-literature.com.

26. Tarbell, Ida M., *A Short Life of Napoleon Bonaparte* (New York: S. S. McClure), 1896. The inaugural issue of the series in McClure's was

volume 3, number 6, November 1894, individual issue cost being 15 cents.

27. Tompkins, Mary E. "Ida M. Tarbell," *American Historians: 1866-1912* in the series *Dictionary of Literary Biography* (Detroit: Gale Research), 1986, p. 297.

28. Ibid.

29. Tompkins, *American Historians*, p. 298-299.

30. "Ida Tarbell," *Twentieth-Century Literary Criticism*, Vol. 40 (Detroit: Gale Research), 1991, p. 421.

31. Tomkins, Mary E., *Ida M. Tarbell* (New York: Twayne Publishers), 1974, pp. 39, 40 and 42. Her entire chapter on "The Uses of Biography: Popular History" is very useful.

32. Tarbell, Ida M., *All in the Day's Work: An Autobiography* (New York: Macmillan), 1939, pp. 148, 150, 153.

33. Tarbell, Ibid., p. 152.

34. Boyd, Kelly, editor, "Napoleonic Wars," *Encyclopaedia of Historians & Historical Writing*, Vol. 2 (London: Fitzroy Dearborn), 1999, p. 852-854; Ellis, Geoffrey, *Napoleon* (London: Longman), 1997, pp. 238-251; Boia, Lucian, *Great Historians of the Modern Age: An International Dictionary* (Westport, Conn.: Greenwood), 1991 and Hughes-Warrington, Marnie, *Fifty Key Thinkers on History* (London: Routledge), 2000.

3: Crafting the Life

1. Catherine Drinker Bowen, *The Writing of Biography*, 1951, p. 30. This small 31-page book was based on a lecture given at Scripps College, Claremont, California, a fascinating account of her five-year experience in writing her biography of John Adams. She discusses not only what information goes into a biography, but also "the shape of what goes into our book" (12). For other inspirations on

biography, see her *Adventures of a Biographer* (1959) and *Biography: The Craft and the Calling* (1969).

2. Although long out of print, Ludwig's *Napoleon* – appearing in a variety of editions including the Modern Library and later condensed by Readers Digest Books – remains easily available in used bookshops and by purchase online. See his *Gifts of Life: A Retrospect* (1931), especially his chapter "My Workshop." Catherine Drinker Bowen, *The Writing of Biography*, p. 8. Meanwhile, I have limited this paper to only books, realizing there other genres of biography such as magazine profiles, films, and plays. And I use the term "authors" in the title, realizing that that some authors of biography may not consider themselves only biographers.

3. Sloane's wonderfully illustrated 1896 leather-bound four-volume *The Life of Napoleon Bonaparte* began as a series of articles published in *The Century Magazine* (1895-1896), and came out in a revised and enlarged library edition in 1910, also four volumes. "Judging from the sales, it has been read by many tens if not hundreds of thousands of readers; and it has been extensively noticed in the critical journals of both worlds," Professor Sloane wrote from New York in the preface to the library edition, p. v. Meanwhile, Tarbell, who published *A Short Life of Napoleon Bonaparte* in 1896, was the author of an issue of *The Mentor* (Vol. 1, No. 38, Nov. 3, 1913) devoted to Napoleon, an 11-page booklet issued from the weekly's Department of Biography.

4. Napoleonic literature is so vast, there could be many genres to include. Writing in his preface to *The Epoch of Napoleon* (New York: Krieger, 1978), Owen Connelly writes from the University of South Carolina that, "Unlike most short 'Napoleon books,' this one is not a biography or military, political, and/or diplomatic history. It has elements of all of these. The emphasis, however, is on Napoleon as civil executive in France and Europe...If it has been done properly, this little book will be of value to students who want the 'word' on Napoleon..." (pp. v-vi). It is interesting to note that his bibliographical note is divided up in the following headings: biographies, life and times, youth/Brumaire, social and economic institutions, warfare, diplomacy, international (with sub-divisions by country), the Bonapartes, other biographies, the last days, and

historiography (pp 174-186). For more about Dr. Connelly, a retired Army lieutenant colonel, see the "Featured Scholar" interview by June K. Burton in *Napoleon* magazine, July 1998, No. 12, pp. 23-31). One example of this genre would be New York University's Leo Gershoy's *The French Revolution and Napoleon* (1933), dedicated to the famous historian Carl Becker.

5. Dodge, preface to volume 3, pp. iv and vi, respectively. The set in my possession, dated 1932 with the copyright renewed by his second wife Clara, had been owned by West Point cadet John S. Samuel, which included a test study sheet on portions of the book by the Department of Engineering course in military history.

6. Dodge, preface to volume 3, p. 150.

7. Dodge, volume four, p. 672.

8. Dupuy, foreword, p. xi.

9. Herold's *The Age of Napoleon* was a Book-of-the-Month Club selection, and subsequently has been re-issued in several paperback editions. His other books include *Mistress to an Age: A Life of Madame de Stael*, which was also a Book-of-the-Month Club selection and winner of the National Book Award; *The Mind of Napoleon*; *Love in Five Temperaments*; *Bonaparte in Egypt*; and *The Battle of Waterloo*.

10. Durant, *A Dual Autobiography*, p. 406. By 1986, Book-of-the-Month Club had distributed 767,789 sets of The Story of Civilization (see Clifton Fadiman's essay about the Durants, "An Appreciation," in *The Book of the Month: Sixty Years of Books in American Life*, edited by Al Silverman (Boston: Little, Brown), 1986, pp. 15-17).

11. Durant, *Age of Napoleon*, p. vii.

12. Durant, *A Dual Autobiography*, p. 388.

13. Durant, *A Dual Autobiography*, pp. 776, 779.

14. Winwar, *Napoleon and the Battle of Waterloo*, pp. 177-178.

15. Manfred Weidhorn, *Napoleon*, p. 4. Read more about the author at his Yeshiva University web page: www.yu.edu/faculty/pages/Weidhorn-Manfred.

16. Marrin, *Napoleon and the Napoleonic Wars*, p. 6. Reference is made to an excerpt from *The Horn Book* review on the first page of the Puffin paperback edition. For more on Marrin, see his website at www.albertmarrin.com.

17. Watson, *Napoleon: A Sketch of His Life, Character, Struggles, and Achievements*, p. ix. For an outline of biographical information, see the entry on Watson in *Who's Who in American History, Vol. 1: 1897-1942* (Chicago: Marquis), 1962, p. 1,309. Watson represented Georgia in the U.S. Senate for one term from 1921-1927.

18. Watson, p. 386 and p. 410.

19. Warwick, p. 449 and p. 437.

20. James Morgan, *In the Footsteps of Napoleon*, pp. 1-2.

21. Morgan, p. 493. Finally, Morgan's approach calls to mind a *National Geographic* cover story in 1982 by John J. Putman, a senior writer for the magazine with photographer Gordon W. Gahan. The team spent four months traveling 30,000 miles and visiting a dozen nations, retracing the footsteps of Napoleon for the 47-page feature: "…seeking to unravel the enigma of his personality, to measure the effect he had in the shaping of modern Europe and France, to see what remains of his legend…In time I would begin to feel his presence: When I arrived someplace, it often seemed as if he had only just departed; the map cases, the portable field bed, the cheap snuff he favored all having been shoved hurriedly into an army wagon moments before it clattered off." John J. Putman, "Napoleon," *National Geographic* (February 1982, Vol. 161, No. 2), pp. 142-189, p. 150 (also see introductory remarks in the "On Assignment" page unnumbered).

22. Walter Geer, *Napoleon the First*, p. v. For an outline of biographical information, see the entry on Geer in *Who's Who in American History*, *Vol. 1: 1897-1942* (Chicago: Marquis), 1962, p. 446.

23. Geer, *Napoleon the First*, p. 357.

24. Geer, *Napoleon and His Family: The Story of a Corsican Clan, Corsica-Madrid*, pp. v-vi.

25. Geer, *Napoleon and Josephine*, p. v.

26. Geer, *Napoleon and Marie-Louise*, p. vi.

27. Albert Guerard, *Napoleon I*, pp. vii-xi. For an outline of biographical information, see the entry on Guerard in *Who's Who in American History*, *Vol. 3: 1951-1960* (Chicago: Marquis), 1963, p. 352. In his sources, he refers to his "American readers" (p. 195) and includes American author William Sloane among the "best known" general works, but gives credit to F.M. Kircheisen's *Napoleon* (1932) as the "most practical" one-volume history and Ludwig's *Napoleon* (1926) as the one which "remains the most readable." (195-196).

28. Guerard, p. 192.

29. Alan Schom, *Napoleon Bonaparte*, pp. xvii-xix, p. 786, p. 789.

30. Robert Asprey, *The Rise of Napoleon Bonaparte*, pp. xvii and xx.

31. J. David Markham, *Napoleon's Road to Glory*, p. 11

32. Markham, *Napoleon for Dummies*, pp.1-2.

33. Steven Englund, *Napoleon: A Political Life*, pp. xiii-xiv. Johns Hopkins' David Bell believes that Englund's work "is by far the best available in English" (*The First Total War: Napoleon's Europe and the Birth of Warfare as We Know It*, Boston: Houghton Mifflin, 2007, p. 343) and one of America's deans of the study of biography, Baruch College's Carl Rollyson agrees, calling it "one of the finest

biographies of Napoleon..." in *Essays in Biography* (Lincoln, Nebraska: iUniverse), 2005, p. 58.

34. Englund, pp. 471, 472.

35. Englund, p. 540.

36. Englund, e-mail to author.

37. David Bell, e-mail to author.

Sources Cited

Robert B. Asprey, *The Rise of Napoleon Bonaparte*, New York: Basic Books, 2000.

-----, *The Reign of Napoleon Bonaparte*, New York: Basic Books, 2001.

Theodore Ayrault Dodge, *Napoleon* (a part of his *History of the Art of War*, a.k.a. the "Great Captains" series), Boston: Houghton Mifflin (original copyright 1904), 1932.

Trevor Nevitt Dupuy, *The Military Life of Napoleon: Emperor of the French*, New York: Franklin Watts, 1969.

Will and Ariel Durant, *The Age of Napoleon: A History of European Civilization from 1789-1815* (Part XI, *The Story of Civilization*), New York: Simon and Schuster, 1975.

-----, *A Dual Autobiography*, New York: Simon and Schuster, 1977.

Philip Dwyer, Napoleon and Biography, *Modern & Contemporary France* (2000), volume 8, no. 4, pp. 520-523.

Steven Englund, *Napoleon: A Political Life*, Cambridge, Mass: Harvard University Press, 2004.

Walter Geer, *Napoleon the First: An Intimate Biography*, New York: Brentano's, 1921.

Leo Gershoy, The French Revolution and Napoleon, New York: Appleton-Century-Crofts, (original copyright 1933), 1961.

Albert Guerard, *Napoleon I: A Great Life in Brief*, New York: Alfred Knopf, 1956.

J. Christopher Herold, *The Age of Napoleon*, New York: American Heritage, 1963.

J. David Markham, *Napoleon's Road to Glory: Triumphs, Defeats, & Immortality*, London: Brassey's, 2003.

-----, *Napoleon for Dummies*, Indianapolis: Wiley Publishing, 2005.

Albert Marrin, *Napoleon and the Napoleonic Wars*, New York: Puffin Books (original copyright 1991), 1993.

Toby McLeod, Napoleonic Scholarship Since the 'Campaigns of Napoleon,' *British Commission for Military History Spring Conference Report*, Lady Margaret Hall, Oxford, May 7, 2005.

James Morgan, *In the Footsteps of Napoleon: His Life and its Famous Scenes*, New York, Macmillan, 1915.

Alan Schom, *Napoleon Bonaparte*, New York: Harper Perennial, 1998.

Thomas E. Watson, *Napoleon: A Sketch of His Life, Character, Struggles, and Achievements*, New York: Dodd, Mead (original copyright 1902), 1926.

Charles F. Warwick, *Napoleon and the End of the French Revolution*, Philadelphia: George W. Jacobs, 1910.

Manfred Weidhorn, *Napoleon*, New York: Atheneum, 1986.

Frances Winwar, *Napoleon and the Battle of Waterloo* (Landmark Books), New York: Random House, 1953.

4: The Publishers

1. E.M. Crane, writing as president of D. Van Nostrand Company, in *A Century of Book Publishing: 1848-1948*, New York: D. Van Nostrand Company, 1948, p. 72. The firm began at 128 Fulton Street, New York (later moving to 192 Broadway) and just prior to the Civil War, became the official publisher for the Army and the Navy, p. 8.

2. For a list of publishers, early titles by publisher, and costs, see O. A. Roorbach, *Catalogue of American Publications Including Reprints and Original Works* 1820-1852 (and supplements and addenda's for later years), New York: Peter Smith, 1939. Crane, Ibid., refers to the close association between publishing, importing, and bookselling as "the three staple activities of the nineteenth century bookman," p. 7. See Adolph Crowoll, *Book Trade Bibliography in the United States in the Nineteenth Century* (New York: Burt Franklin), for early bookseller organizations and efforts by publishers to improve on the quality of printing ink and paper.

3. John Tebbel, *A History of Book Publishing in the United States: The Creation of an Industry 1630-1865*, volume one, New York: R.R. Bowker, 1972, pp. 221-222. He also wrote that, "America's drive toward universal literacy...produced in the 1840s the largest reading audience anyone had ever seen. This audience virtually demanded books..."p. 207. Tebbel also tells us that the "technological explosion" in printing before the Civil War (especially from 1825-1850) – making modern book publishing possible – consisted of the flatbed press, then the cylinder press, replacing the wooden-screw type hand press. p. 257.

4. Crane, Ibid., continuing, "Already in friendly association with the leaders of the young Army hierarchy, the new firm (D. Van Nostrand Company) imported books in both categories – professional military treatises from England and France for army use and historical studies for the layman," p. 5.

5. Tebbel, Ibid., who continues, "...soon to be overtaken...by both New York and Boston," p. 203. See Tebbel's section on Philadelphia publishers, pp. 365-386.

6. Tebbel, Ibid., p. 369. Carey publishers also published all of Jane Austen's novels in uniform editions of 1,250 copies, p. 370.

7. See Tebbel's section on the Carey firm. He includes an interesting list of the progression of firm names after being founded in 1785 by Mathew Carey: Carey, Stewart & Co., 1787; M. Carey & Son, 1817; M. Carey & Sons, 1821; Carey & Lea, 1824; Carey, Lea, & Carey, 1826; Carey, Lea & Blanchard, 1833; Lea & Blanchard, 1836; Blanchard & Lea, 1851; Henry C. Lea, 1865; Henry C. Lea's Son & Co., 1880; Lea Brothers & Co., 1885; and Lea & Febiger, 1908, p. 366. See Robert E. Robinson, *William Hazlitt's Life of Napoleon Bonaparte: It's Sources and Characteristics*, Geneva: Droz, 1959.

8. Other Philadelphia publishers of Napoleon titles included the Carey & Hart's three-volume Hazlitt at $3; this house was the publisher of the best-seller *Life of David Crockett* in 1833. A. [Abraham] Hart houses' *Napoleon and The Marshals of the Empire* in two volumes at $2 published between 1820-1852.

9. Headley's *Napoleon and His Marshals* is mentioned as a best-seller for 1846 in Richard B. Morris, *Encyclopedia of American History* (New York: Harper & Brothers, 1953), which included continued sales "after their period, including cheap reprints," p. 566. According to Roger Burlingame, *Of Making Many Books: A Hundred Years of Reading, Writing, and Publishing* (New York: Charles Scribner's Sons, 1946), J. T. Headley's *Napoleon* and *Washington* sets "within a year...had been written, printed, bound, and put on the counters and that ultimate sales of these books passed the quarter million mark," p. 57. Baker and Scribner was also the publisher of Charlotte Elizabeth's works, 28 titles on their list by 1847, selling for 25 to 60 cents each. Of course, this house would become Charles Scribner's Sons, also publishers of Scribner's Magazine (1886), Scribner's Monthly (1870), and St. Nicholas (a juvenile magazine in 1871), see Hellmut Lehmann-Haupt, *The Book in America: A History of the Making and Selling of Books in the United States* (New York: R. R. Bowler Company, 1951), pp. 222-223.

10. Tebbel, Ibid., p. 316.

11. Hellmut Lehman-Haupt (in collaboration with Lawrence C. Wroth and Rollo G. Silver), *The Book in America: A History of the Making and Selling of Books in the United States* (New York: R. R. Bowler Company, 1951), p. 217. Harpers began *Harper's Magazine* in 1850, adding *Harper's Weekly* (1857), *Harper's Bazaar* (1867), and *Harper's Young People* (1879), p. 218. For prices on Abbott's books, see Roorbach.

12. William Milligan Sloane, professor of History at Columbia University, in the preface to the library edition of *The Life of Napoleon Bonaparte* (New York: The Century Co., 1912 edition of the 1910 issue), p. v of Vol. I.

13. Brentano's published a volume edited and translated by Geer a year earlier, in 1920, *Recollections of the Revolution and The Empire*, with 15 "photogravure" illustrations, all with tissue.

5: American Best-Seller

1. Stephen B. Oates, *Readings in Biography: An Annotated, Selective Guide* (copyrighted manuscript), 1988, p. 18. He wrote this paper with the assistance of Karen Manners Smith. At the time, Oates was Paul Murray Kendall Professor of Biography and Professor of History at the University of Massachusetts, Amherst. Smith, a graduate of Professor Oate's graduate seminar in life-writing and his research assistant, was then a Ph.D. candidate in history at the University of Massachusetts, Amherst.

2. *The New Yorker*, January 15, 1927, p. 66.

3. For best-seller listings, see Alice Payne Hackett, *70 Years of Best Sellers, 1895-1965* (New York, R. R. Bowker Company, 1967). One American edition of his *Napoleon* sold 400,000 copies. Other best-selling biographies over the years include those by Felix Markham, Vincent Cronin, and Alan Schom.

4. Leo Gershoy, *The French Revolution and Napoleon* (New York: Appleton-Century-Crofts,1933), p. 554; A. M. Schom, letter, February 7, 2011.

5. David A. Bell, e-mail, February 17, 2011.

6. "Emil Ludwig" in *Twentieth Century Authors: A Biographical Dictionary of Modern Literature*, pp. 858-859, edited by Stanley J. Kunitz and Howard Haycraft, New York: The H. W. Wilson Company, 1942; "Emil Ludwig" in *World Authors: 1900-1950* (The Wilson Authors Series), pp. 1,619-1,620, Vol. 3, Editors Martin Seymour-Smith and Andrew C. Kimmens, New York/Dublin: The H. W. Wilson Company, 1996; W. N. Hargreaves-Mawdsley, *Everyman's Dictionary of European Writers*, pp. 335-336, London: Dent/New York: Dutton, 1968. His other biographies translated into English include Bismarck (1927), Wilhelm Hohenzollern (1927), Goethe (1928), Jesus (1928 and revised edition 1957), Lincoln (1929, reissued 1949, and abridged 1956), Schliemann 1931), Hindenburg (1935), Masaryk (1936), Cleopatra (1937), Franklin Roosevelt (1938), Bolivar (1942), Stalin (1942), Beethoven (1943), and Mackensie King (1944), along with several works featuring groups of individuals. He also wrote about places (the Nile and the Mediterranean) and published plays and novels.

7. Ludwig, *Gifts of Life: A Retrospect*, edited by Ethel Colburn Mayne, translated from the German by M. I. Robertson (Boston: Little, Brown, and Company), 1931. As in his biographies, he divided his own autobiographical reflection into books or stages. *Gifts of Life* consisted of three: Romanticism, Metamorphosis, and Middle Life. Reflecting on when he was working on his play about Napoleon, he wrote of Napoleon, "I had convinced myself that he was half a dreamer, half a mathematician, as much visionary as practical man, and thus could reduce him to my formula of artist and man of the world. I so depicted him in a five-act play, showing that his downfall was caused by this duality, this breach of continuity," p. 144.

8. Ludwig, *Genius and Character*, translated by Kenneth Burke (New York: Blue Ribbon Books), 1927. See the introduction, "On the Writing of History." The book features profiles of Frederick the Great, Baron Vom Stein, Bismarck, Stanley, Peters, Rhodes, Wilson, Rathenau, Lenin, Leonardo da Vinci, Shakespeare, Rembrandt's Self-Portrait, Voltaire in Eighteen Tableaux, Lord Byron and LaSalle, Goethe and Schiller, Dehmel, Balzac, and Portrait of an Officer

(Gott erhalte Franz den Kaiser). Plutarch quoted in the introduction by James Atlas in *Plutarch's Lives*, Vol. I, the Dryden Translation, edited with notes and preface by Arthur Hugh Clough, paperback edition, Modern Library: New York, 2001, pp. xiii-xiv.

9. Ludwig, *Genius and Character*, pp. 8-9.

10. Ludwig, concluding section of *Napoleon*, "Envoy," pp. 679-682.

11. Ludwig *Napoleon* references are from the 14th large edition translated by Eden and Cedar Paul (New York: Boni Liveright, 1928, originally published 1926): St. Helena passage, pp. 547, 620. This edition was printed by Quinn & Boden Company, Inc., Rahway, New Jersey.

12. Ludwig, ibid, history passage, p. 64.

13. Ludwig, ibid, maps passage, p. 336.

14. Albert Guerard, *Napoleon I: A Great Life in Brief* (New York: Knopf, 1956), p. 196; Steven Englund, Napoleon: A Political Life (Cambridge, Mass: Harvard University Press, 2004), p. 473; J. David Markham, e-mail, January 23, 2011.

15. Ambrose, Academy of Achievement, Museum of Living History, Washington, D.C., interview, May 22, 1998, p. 3: www.achievement.org/autodoc/printmember/amb0int-1; Connelly, "A Maverick Talks Horse Sense," interview by June K. Burton, *Napoleon* magazine, No. 12, July 1998; Horward, "Napoleon and Wellington," interview by June K. Burton, *Napoleon* magazine, No. 11, February 1998.

16. Marston Balch, *Modern Short Biography & Autobiography*, (New York: Harcourt Brace & Co.), 1935, pp. 411-412.

17. Donald J. Winslow, *Life-Writing: A Glossary of Terms in Biography, Autobiography, and Related Forms* (Honolulu: University of Hawaii Press, 1980), pp. 37, 43.

18. Ruth Hoberman, in "Biography: General Survey," in *Encyclopedia of Life Writing: Autobiographical and Biographical Forms*, Vol. I, A-K, editor, Margaretta Jolly (London Chicago: Fitzroy Dearborn Publishers, 2001), pp. 109-112. She also references Ludwig in her section on "New Biography" in Vol. 2, saying how "this 'new school' came to be known as 'the new biography." According to Hoberman, "Reaching a peak during the 1920s and 1930s, the new biography was defined by its emphasis on the subject's inner life and by its attempt at stylistic brilliance," with typical examples including Strachey's Queen Victoria, Ludwig's Goethe, Nicholson's Tennyson, Maurois's Ariel, Scott's The Portrait of Zelide, and Cecil's The Stricken Deer or the Life of Cowper," p. 650.

19. Hermione Lee, *Biography: A Very Short Introduction* (Oxford University Press, 2009), p. 79; Edgar Johnson, *One Mighty Torrent: The Drama of Biography* (New York: The Macmillian Company, 1955), p. 480; and Carl Rollyson, *Biography: A User's Guide* (Chicago: Ivan R. Dee, 2008), p. 210.

20. Felix E. Hirsch, "Memories of Emil Ludwig," *Books Abroad: An International Literary Quarterly*, Vol. 23, University of Oklahoma Press, 1949, pp. 113-118. Hirsch was professor of History and a librarian at Bard College and later at Trenton State College.

21. *Gifts of Life*, p. 436. "Dogs were my refuge," Ludwig wrote (p. 187). "The influence of dogs in our lives grew stronger and stronger, and I should not like ever to be without them" (p. 213).

22. Ludwig's *Napoleon*, p. 681-682.

6: Teaching Napoleon

1. Ida M. Tarbell in the foreword of *The Story of Napoleon* by Mabell S.C. Smith, New York: Thomas Y. Crowell Company, 1928, pp. v and vi.

2. Rafe Blaufarb, *Napoleon: Symbol for an Age: A Brief History with Documents* (The Bedford Series in History and Culture), Boston/New York: Bedford/St. Martin's, p.2.

3. Professor Judith Stone, e-mail, Feb. 3, 2008.

4. Professor David Barclay, e-mail, Feb. 8, 2008.

3. Steven L. Delvaux, e-mail, August 29, 2000. While discussing charisma, he also wrote: "The bottom line is that he understood, not just soldiers, but human nature, exemplifying what the U.S. Army of today considers to be one of the principles of leadership: 'Know your soldiers and look out for their well-being.' While we may not be able to teach the intangible characteristics of charisma, we can certainly identify and attempt to emulate the more tangible qualities outlined above which were such important components of Napoleon's leadership."

In discussing Napoleon's professionalism, he adds: "The success he achieved during the First Italian Campaign (1796-97) and at Marengo, Ulm, Austerlitz, Jena-Auerstadt, etc., was not a matter of being lucky, but rather being good. Critics have countered that his victories were in some aspects a matter of blundering to glory. But in fact, Napoleon created his own luck. He was able to shape the battlefield toward the desired outcome. He had a vision, and he was almost always able to make his vision a reality on the field of battle because of his limitless knowledge and understanding of warfare. His most magnificent battle, Austerlitz, is perhaps the best example of this. He set up the Austro-Russian force to perform in a certain way, and when they did, he crushed them. All of which, I emphasize, Napoleon provides us with a perfect illustration of the benefit of learning from the lessons of history."

4. E. L. Bowie, e-mail, September 7, 2000. His response also included: "Within the Military History general course, four separate lessons are devoted in whole or part to Napoleon's legacy. While "modern" warfare in its current U.S. Army definition is regarded as having begun some 200 years before the rise of Napoleon, it is with Napoleonic warfare that most students begin to see recognizably familiar military organization and concept. The Division, The Corps, the mass army, and the overwhelming majority of operational terms and concepts still in use had their origin with Napoleon and/or the times he shaped."

5. Mike Matheny, e-mail, September 1, 2000. Colonel Matheny further wrote: "From the Peloponnesian Wars to Desert Storm there is an amazing consistency in human strategic behavior. Whether we use bows and arrows or M1 tanks, at the strategic level nations seek to successfully match strategy and policy – to balance ends, ways, and means to achieve their objectives and protect vital interests. Napoleonic France's struggle with Great Britain is a classic case study of a Continental power trying to come to grips with a maritime power. Napoleon's faith in his military genius led to an obsession with operational solutions to strategic problems, and ultimately strategic over-reach. He constantly sought to substitute tactical success for sound strategy. This is strikingly similar to the German's approach to warfare throughout most of the 20th century. The 20 years of warfare which consumed Europe and changed the face of the world can provide the reflective student with many insights – rich perspectives on the nature of war, theory and strategy."

ACKNOWLEDGEMENTS

The Michigan Academy of Science, Arts & Letters for the opportunities to research and present these presentations…

Dr. Mike Moskovis and Dot Selinger (my honorary research assistants) for sending me more than a decade worth of clippings, booklets, exhibit programs and many other important treasures …

Daughter and son-in-law Kelly and Rob Knecht for my most-prized volumes, the first American edition (1827) of Sir Walter Scott's *The Life of Napoleon Bonaparte* in three volumes, published by Carey, Lea & Carey of Philadelphia…

My brother Dave and friends – author Dave Dempsey, Lt. Col. Don Mercer (Ret.), and historian Steve Rossio – who encouraged me in my research and writing and (without knowing it) helped motivate me to assemble this collection…

Friends like Dr. John and Debbie Sinclair and Dr. Pete and Pam McFarlane who added to my collection of old and rare Napoleon books and an assortment of collectables over many years…

Rebecca Sinclair who brought a young Napoleon Bonaparte to life for our cover, while celebrating the contribution of an earlier American artist, James Fagan…

Tom Coyne for assisting with the preparation of this revised edition…

Biographer Linda Davis for many years of encouragement in writing and publishing and fellow bibliophile Daryl Longman for listening as I developed some of these themes while visiting his bookshop…

The many French III students in the classes of Sara Heil who endured my ramblings at Portage Public Schools, along with my colleagues there who listened patiently (sometimes) to my research findings and observations as I prepared for my Michigan Academy presentations…

The friendly people at CreateSpace, an Amazon Company, who made this publishing process so easy…

And – again – to my wife Kathy (there will be a cruise!), along with family and friends who know more about Napoleon in America than they really needed to know.

Visit the author on Linked-in:
www.linkedin.com/pub/tom-vance/59/982/248/

Made in the USA
Charleston, SC
31 October 2015